Equality In Diversity

By

Joseph Gilson (BD)

All rights reserved, including the right to reproduce this book, or portions thereof in any form. No part of this text may be reproduced, transmitted, downloaded, decompiled, reverse engineered, or stored, in any form or introduced into any information storage and retrieval system, in any form or by any means, whether electronic or mechanical without the express written permission of the author.

ISBN:

I certify that all the material in this work which is not my own is duly acknowledged.

Signature: ……………………………

Dedication page

This book is dedicated to all those who have suffered inequality and discrimination because of their Gender, Sexuality Orientation, Age, Religion, National Origin, Pregnancy and many others and to my best friend and son Aaron.

Table of contents
1. Preface
2. Epigraph
3. Foreword
4. Introduction
5 Defining Racism.
6. The demographics, regimes, and approaches races
7. Inequality within UK and the USA
8. The Black lives movement
9. Meghan Markle and British racism
10. Inequality in Zimbabwe
11. Racism in America
12. Inequality and racism in South Africa
13. Immigration and diversity
14. Legislation, Equality and Diversity.
15. Disability Discrimination Act 1995,
16. The Human Rights Act 1998,
17 The Schools Standards and Framework Act 1998
18. The Care Standards Act 2000
19. The Equality Act 2010 and UN Convention
20. Nelson Mandela and the antidiscrimination policy
21. Equal opportunity
22. When discrimination is ok
23. Conclusion
24. Acknowledgements
25. About the Author
25. Footnotes
27. Bibliography

Epigraph

"'I have a dream that my four little children will one day live in a nation where they will not be judged by the color of their skin but by the content of their character.'[1]

---

[1] Pep Talk , *Master the Art of Public Speaking.* India.2020,35

Preface

The information contained in this book is presented solely for general educational purposes; as we might know that knowledge is power, and this represents a historical documentation of the traditional medicine practices used. The Author of the book accepts no personal liability for any inappropriate use of the information presented in this book.

Foreword

As a dear friend and colleague, I know Chaplain Joseph Gilson to be a conscientious and loving man who displays the compassion and grace the Son of God and our Lord Jesus Christ commissioned us to show one another.

Obtaining his BD degree in Theology and the challenges he faced as a young man growing up in Africa enables him to identify, minister and care for people from different spheres and ethnicity. With many years of Pastoral experience, and love for the Scriptural Truth of the Bible, Chaplain Gilson furthermore, brings the message of hope to those in times of suffering and hopelessness during the unprecedented times of the Covid-19 pandemic.

Trinitarian Blessings
Sharon Connolly

Theological Studies BA (UHI)

In this book it is my desire not only to advocate for equality and diversity but also to highlight the global response to racism, the dilemma that transcends through generations of the entire world. Equality and diversity implementation means that rational and accessible services are made available for everyone. This creates a safe and inclusive atmosphere that celebrates difference and valuing everyone as well as ensuring that all people can be treated equal with respect and dignity in a consistent way challenging discrimination and harassment committed against every human being. The aim is to break down unnecessary barriers for every human being seeking opportunities of progress in everyday life and to demonstrate the principles of diversity and inclusion in people's daily activities, functions and roles.

Introduction

With the growing population, it has become a great challenge to maintain the equality in our diverse world. It is important to know that each individual is unique despite our different ethnicity, race, socio-economic status, age, gender, sexual orientation physical abilities, political beliefs, religious beliefs, or any other ideologies. Diversity is about discovering these differences in a positive, safe and nurturing environment. It is about considering each other and progressing beyond mere tolerance to accepting and celebrating the rich magnitudes of diversity hidden within each one of us. Diversity is not only recognising the differences but knowing how to relate with people of different race, gender, class, physical abilities, as well as religious status and many others.

Definition of Racism

Albet asserts: '(This definition, "What Is Racism?," is reprinted in Appendix B.) This definition also laid greater emphasis on the doctrinal basis of racist attitudes (their connection with biological theories of race, which he calls "raciology") while still pointing to the more general range of phenomena encompassed in his earlier definition, which he now called "ethnophobia."'[2] This demonstrates that racism can be connected to biological theories about race.

Racism can signify antagonism towards other people who have different looks or who differ in their expression of worship. Webster proclaims: 'The term ' racism ' is often used in discussions of crime and criminal justice to refer to different and discriminatory treatment of

---

[2] Memmi Albert. *Racism*. (Minneapolis: University of Minnesota Press 1999)10

individuals and groups by the police and criminal justice system on grounds of their supposed racial background.'[3] This gives us the idea that some people can be discriminated even by the police and the criminal justice only because of their racial background. Webster goes on to say that: 'As already mentioned, it cannot be assumed that all racism and discrimination is perpetrated by whites on blacks or other minorities. Neither is the existence of some significant minority crime a myth, although the belief that a lot of crime is perpetrated by minorities on whites is a myth.'[4] This indicates that stereotyping leads to the assumption that the white people are racists or that the black people are the crime perpetrators.

Albert asserts: 'In Memmi's exposition, racism is a charge, like a judicial accusation, levied against another, who is metaphorically indicted for being in some manner (racially) different.'[5] This means that racism can be the victim's interpretation of injustice by the dominant one. This may mean that the racist may not notice racism but the victim of racism. In another way it may not be real but a feeling of injustice from the victim due to their difference from the dominant. Albert further declares: 'The indictment, however, is unfounded and wholly unjust, and the accused is thus the victim of an injustice (of being accused and derogated).'[6] This means that the accused may suffer for being different and not necessarily for being guilty of racism. Sometimes racism is how the victim feels like rather than rather than the actual act of

---

[3]Colin Webster *Understanding Race and Crime.* Buckingham: McGraw-Hill Education. 2007)3
[4]Colin Webster *Understanding Race and Crime.* Buckingham: McGraw-Hill Education. 2007)6
[5]Memmi Albert. Racism.29
[6]Memmi Albert. Racism.29

racism. By this I mean that it is possible for a racist to be unaware of their practice until it is highlighted by the victim of racism.

Yanco draws from King: 'There must be a recognition on the part of everybody in this nation that America is still a racist country. Now however unpleasant that sounds, it is the truth. And we will never solve the problem of racism until there is a recognition of the fact that racism still stands at the centre of so much of our nation and we must see racism for what it is. Martin Luther King Jr., from "The Other America," address delivered at Grosse Pointe, Michigan, March 1968'[7] This means that it is impossible to solve a problem by denying that it exists but we can solve a problem only when we acknowledge that it exists and confront it to change it. It is easy to cover up and deny the fact that the minority suffers discrimination in our nations although it is done in a very hidden and clever way like not building wheel chair access in some of our buildings as a way of avoiding wheel chair users.

Racism can come in different forms. Stefan asserts: 'In 1963, historian Mark Haller stated in the first monograph about eugenics in the United States that "between the mid-1920s and 1940 racism ceased to have scientific respectability, and as a result American eugenics and racism faced a parting of the ways." The idea of racial superiority survived only among "innumerable right-wing anti-semitic groups and among white supremacists" in the United States.'[8] This appears to be a hidden way of

---

[7] Yanco, Jennifer J... *Misremembering Dr. King : Revisiting the Legacy of Martin Luther King Jr.* (Bloomington: Indiana University Press. 2014)51

[8] Kuhl, Stefan. *The Nazi Connection : Eugenics, American Racism, and*

exterminating a race just as Hitler devised Holocaust as a way of getting rid of the Jewish people. Piontek asserts: 'The concept of depopulation derives directly from eugenics, which was dynamically developing in the USA before World War II and was implemented
and developed by Nazi Germany.' [9] This may indicate that the US and the Nazi Germany were involved in the crimes against humanity. Making people sterile is obvious a way of destroying human kind by stopping humans from reproducing themselves. This appears diabolic as it contradicts the plan of God .Genesis 1:28 (NIV) 'God blessed them and said to them, "Be fruitful and increase in number; fill the earth and subdue it..'[10] This proves that it was God's plan for humans to be productive.

Piontek continues : 'Depopulation trends are characterized by an approach that takes away human subjectivity and a special place and function, determined by the Creator that makes the Earth subject to themselves'[11] Depopulation may assume that the earth is more valuable than humans. Piontek asserts further : 'The proposed remedy to the identified risks is a global fertility reduction

---

German National Socialism. Cary: Oxford University Press,2002)xiv
[9] Wojciech Piontek 2019 Depopulation in the Concept of Sustainable Development Middle Pomeranian scientific Society Of Environment Protection Rocznik Ochrona Środowiska (Online) Paper Volume 21 (Pp 523-542 Available:
https://ros.edu.pl/images/roczniki/2019/032_ROS_V21_R2019.pdf
Accessed:12/01/2021
[10] Genesis 1:28
[11]Wojciech Piontek 2019 Depopulation in the Concept of Sustainable Development Middle Pomeranian scientific Society Of Environment Protection Rocznik Ochrona Środowiska (Online) Paper Volume 21 (Pp 524 Available:
https://ros.edu.pl/images/roczniki/2019/032_ROS_V21_R2019.pdf
Accessed:12/01/2021

strategy (Kissinger 1974, p. 74), based on the promotion of lifestyles alternative to parenthood, the development of contraception (Kissinger 1974, p. 110) and the assurance and promotion of abortion as a basic human right (Kissinger 1974, p. 114-120).'[12] Although not true this may suggest that the vaccination programme against the Covid 19 Corona virus may be part of the plan of depopulation considering the after effects of the kind of medications used.. Kintsurashvili asserts: 'Bill Gates' involvement in the development of a vaccine against the coronavirus was assessed by "Georgia and World" as dangerous and was linked to the public address of Bill Gates in 2010. In 2010, Bill Gates gave a speech "Innovating to zero" at Ted Talks, in which he spoke about reduction of CO_2 emissions and noted that vaccination may play a significant role in terms of population growth control.

Bill Gates: "The world today has 6.8 billion people. That's headed up to about 9 billion. Now, if we do a really great job on new vaccines, health care, reproductive health services, we could lower that [population growth rate] by, perhaps 10 or 15 percent".

"Georgia and World" used the quote without taking into account the context, and concluded that Bill Gates was trying to lower human ability to reproduce and consequently, to reduce human population.'[13] Bill Gates

---

[12] Wojciech Piontek 2019 Depopulation in the Concept of Sustainable Development Middle Pomeranian scientific Society Of Environment Protection Rocznik Ochrona Środowiska (Online) Paper Volume 21 (Pp 523-542 Available:
https://ros.edu.pl/images/roczniki/2019/032_ROS_V21_R2019.pdf
Accessed:12/01/2021

[13] Tamar Kintsurashvili , Maiko Ratiani 30 April 2020 Does Bill Gates promise us depopulation and chipping? Healthcare/Biosafety Online

may have been misunderstood as his aim may be to slow population growth, rather than reducing the population. Kintsurashvili elaborates: 'Gates notes that vaccines are crucial for reduction of child mortality in the developing countries, which, for its part, will slow population growth, according to Bill Gates. More specifically, Bill Gates thinks that when more children survive, parents will choose to have fewer children. Women will have a number of children they can support, send them to school and take care about their health, which is a precondition for overcoming poverty and improving living standards. As for the carbon dioxide emissions, according to Bill Gates, reducing the world population growth will also reduce CO_2 emissions. Accordingly, vaccines are not directed against the world's population. Bill and Melinda Gates have been talking about this since 2009.'[14] The word 'directed' may be a clue that vaccines are not focussed against world population although its side effects may be fatal to human reproduction. This also proves that vaccine are mainly targeted the developing countries where human population is much higher than in the first world countries. If vaccine has negative results to a specific race then this may suggest a hidden way of racial discrimination.

---

article .Available: http://www.mythdetector.ge/en/myth/does-bill-gates-promise-us-depopulation-and-chipping Accessed: 12/01/2021

[14]Tamar Kintsurashvili , Maiko Ratiani 30 April 2020 Does Bill Gates promise us depopulation and chipping? Healthcare/Biosafety Online article .Available: http://www.mythdetector.ge/en/myth/does-bill-gates-promise-us-depopulation-and-chipping Accessed: 12/01/2021

Due to fear, hesitation and mistrust black people appear to be more hesitant to take to vaccines against the Covid 19 .Warren asserts: 'What are the barriers to greater participation of Black people in Covid-19 trials? Although they are multiple, a critical factor is the deep and justified lack of trust that many Black Americans have for the health care system in general and clinical research in particular. This distrust is often traced to the legacy of the infamous syphilis study at Tuskegee, in which investigators withheld treatment from hundreds of Black men in order to study the natural history of the disease. But the distrust is far more deeply rooted, in centuries of well-documented examples of racist exploitation by American physicians and researchers.'[15] This explains how historical racism and discrimination has caused the black community to remain suspicious of any tools that has the potential of being used against race.

The demographics, regimes, and approaches of racial and ethnic groups

The New Strategist asserts: 'Understanding the demographics, lifestyles, and attitudes of racial and ethnic groups is of vital importance to researchers and policymakers. Racial and Ethnic Diversity provides the key to understanding both the similarities and differences among non-Hispanic whites, blacks, Hispanics, Asians,

---

[15] Rueben C. Warren, D.D.S., Dr.P.H., M.Div., Lachlan Forrow, M.D., David Augustin Hodge, Sr., D.Min., Ph.D., and Robert D. Truog, M.D. 16 Oct 2020 Trustworthiness before Trust — Covid-19 Vaccine Trials and the Black The New England Journal of Medicine (Online) Available: https://www.nejm.org/doi/full/10.1056/NEJMp2030033 Accessed: 12/01/2021

and American Indians. Whenever possible, the tables in Racial and Ethnic Diversity include data that allow researchers to compare characteristics across racial groups.'[16] This means that it helps to study the demographics, regimes, and approaches of racial and ethnic groups for the understanding of both the similarities and differences among different races of people as it allows investigators to compare characteristics across racial groups. At times the subject of equality is often neglected as it appears to be a very sensitive subject

Referring to the American policy Borman asserts: 'Bush was straightforward in his view of equality in elementary and secondary education: everyone is to be held to the same standards, because anything else underestimates the capacity of poor and otherwise disadvantaged children.'[17] This is an indication that Bush prioritised dealing with the inequality which had ever since dominated the schools of America.

Inequality within UK, The National Health Services and USA

Likupe asserts: 'Thirty nurses from sub-Saharan countries working in four NHS trusts were interviewed between 2006 and 2008 using semistructured interviews and focus group discussions to gain an insight into their experiences in the NHS. This study suggests that Black African nurses experienced discrimination and racism

---

[16] The New Strategist Editors, ed. *Racial and Ethnic Diversity : Asians, Blacks, Hispanics, Native Americans and Whites.* (Amityville: New Strategist Press,2013)2

[17] Kathryn Borman, M., and Dorn, Sherma (eds. *Education Reform in Florida : Diversity and Equity in Public Policy.* Ithaca: State University of New York Press. 2007)10

from White colleagues and other overseas nurses, managers, and patients and their relatives as well as lack of opportunities in their workplaces. Managers seemed to treat British and other overseas nurses more favorably than Black African nurses.'[18]This means that the black African nurses were suffering from discrimination and inequality within the NHS. In the United Kingdom to tackle this kind of inequality we should refer to the legislations which are meant to safeguard the disadvantaged as Lockwood, Henderson and Thornicroft asserts: 'The Equality Act 2010 brought all the grounds of discrimination into one statute, harmonised definitions and concepts, and introduced new requirements and concepts. It permits greater scope for positive action, provides expressedly for discrimination based on more than one characteristic, and strengthens disability protections.'[19] This means that the Equality Act 2010 aims to promote equality and to prevent discrimination. Despite all the attempts to give each and every one a fair opportunity, there are still some who tactfully practice discrimination and still get away with it without getting their hands dirty.[20] Henze, Katz, Norte, Sather and Walker asserts: 'The influence of racism is still clearly visible to most people of colour, who can usually name recent incidents in which

---

[18] Gloria Likupe PhD, MSc, PGCEA, BSc (Hons), DipN, RN Uduak Archibong PhD, FWACN, FRCN(Black African Nurses' Experiences of Equality, Racism, and Discrimination in the National Health Service)(Psychological issues in Organisational culture) Wiley Online Library (Oneline)Journal.(Volume3, IssueS1)(Pages 227-246) Available:(https://doi.org/10.1002/jpoc.21071) accessed:14/11/20
[19]Graeme Lockwood , Claire Henderson and Graham Thornicroft (March 2012)(Article/equality-act-2010-and-mental-health) The British Journal of Psychiatry (Online)(Volume 200 , Issue 3,(pp. 182 – 183)Available:DOI: https://doi.org/10.1192/bjp.bp.111.097790) accessed: 01/01/2021
[20] Emphasis: Mine

they felt they were targeted in some way because of their race or ethnicity.'[21] This elaborates that despite the fact that it is now illegal to practice racism in the form of slavery; people are still experiencing racial discrimination in their everyday life experiences.

Pendleton declares: 'Evidence suggests that black and minority ethnic (BME) midwives are more likely to face fitness to practise hearings than white registrants and BME NHS staff are less likely to be in senior positions.'[22] Racial discrimination is an unfair situation in which the black and minority ethnic midwifes finds themselves in. Life doesn't have to be that way as times have long changed allowing the global population to live peacefully together as a united community. When I relocated to the UK , I worked for a certain company in Sheffield where I faced a lot of discrimination from my work colleagues. We shared the same staff room for our breaks. I used one of the company cups for a cup of tea but as I finished I using it one of the work colleagues reached out for that cup and smashed it on the floor as a sign of anger that I had used it. We cannot dispute that these are the challenges that the black people and the other ethnic minority face on a daily basis at their work places despite the fact that there are laws and regulations which are put in place to safeguard all people against any discrimination.

---

[21]Rosemary Henze, Anne Katz Edmundo Norte, Susan E Sather and Ernest Walker. *Leading For Diversity* (Sage Publications Company. London 2002)21

[22] John Pendleton (The experiences of black and minority ethnic nurses working in the UK) British Journal of Nursing (Jan 2017) (Online) (VOL. 26, NO. 1) Available: https://doi.org/10.12968/bjon.2017.26.1.37 Accessed:14/11/20

It is very common that most people who have relocated to the United Kingdom fail to pursue their same trade of profession because they fail to meet the standards of the same profession in their new country of residence. Many of them end up taking health care jobs which are front line jobs with a high risk of infections like the Coved 19 Corona virus. This could be the reason most blacks and other ethnic minority people appeared to be severely affected by the pandemic in early 2020. Drawing from the works of Cheng and Monnat (PhD) : 'Since early March, the average daily increase in the COVID-19 mortality rate has been significantly higher in rural counties with the highest percent Black and Hispanic populations.'[23] This indicates that the black and Hispanic community were severely affected by the coved 19 due to poor living conditions. It possible that due to poverty the blacks and other ethnic minority people are left without a choice but to take those jobs which a considered as the high risky jobs and as a result they are severely hit by the Corona virus.

Byrne, Alexander, Khan, Nazro and Shankley assert: ' The UN Special Rapporteur , reporting in 2018 found 'striking' levels of 'structural socio-economic exclusion of racial and ethnic communities in the UK' as well as ' growth in the acceptability of explicit racial, ethnic and religious intolerance'. Racism and prejudicial attitudes and practices, while improving, in some ways persist, with Muslims and Gypsy-Traveller community in particular facing high levels of prejudice. Acts of bias, discrimination and racial violence remain a pervasive

---

[23] Dyer O.(07 September 2020) (Covid-19: Black people and other minorities are hardest hit in US).The journal of rural health.Online:(Volume36, Issue4) (Pp 602-608)Available: https://doi.org/10.1111/jrh.12511 Accessed:02/01/2021

feature of everyday life for ethnic and religious minority groups, evident in hurtful statements, and forms of aggression, bullying and harassment.'[24] This show how the minority in the UK experience racial abuse on a daily basis from their work places, schools and even from the people who are supposed to safeguard people from abuse like the Police. From my own experience as a person of colour driving a Mercedes Benz car, I could be stopped and searched by the police about three times a day and asked the same question about type of job I do to afford an expensive car. This appears to be racism and prejudicial attitudes to assume that all black people are likely to sell illegal drugs.

Cheng and Monnat asserts further: 'Blacks are also more likely to work in service occupations that require face-to-face contact with customers and are more likely than Whites to live in multigenerational homes and with extended kin, conditions that reduce the ability to socially distance and increase the risk of disease transmission'[25] This proves that it is not because of their poor genetic immune system that the blacks die of the Coved 19 Virus but the reason is the system of living in which they are subjected to which gives them no other choice but live in over populated shared houses where they cannot afford social distance and to take care jobs that require them to be face to face with a service user. Further to my own experience I have worked part time in the healthcare

---

[24] Bridget Byrne, Claire Alexander, Omar Khan, James Nazro and William Shankley *Ethnicity and Race in the UK: State of the Nation* (Bristol University Press, Policy Press 2020)10

[25] Dyer O.(07 September 2020) (Covid-19: Black people and other minorities are hardest hit in US).The journal of rural health.Online:(Volume36, Issue4) (Pp 602-608)Available: https://doi.org/10.1111/jrh.12511 Accessed:02/01/2021

sector and I experienced a situation that whenever there was a service user found to be infected with the Coved 19 Corona virus, It was the Black and the Asian nurses who were assigned to work in that particular unity while our fellow white colleagues worked in the safe environment which were less infected and this is what inspired me to write this book.

Pal elaborates about the situation of the black people and other ethnic minority who live in Glasgow: 'In March 2009, Atkinson opened a whites only pub in the Glasgow area, claiming ' it will be a place where all white people will be welcome apart from the reds and other white scum'. Atkinson said: ' It will be the only place in this country that will go back to the good old days of the colour bar and the non-white will definitely NOT be welcome.'. He told supporters that they are looking to open more such pubs all over the country.'[26] This indicates that Atkinson openly practised racism by having a pub where black people and others from the ethnic minority were not allowed in. It is quite surprising how he got his licence to open such a place during this day and age with all anti-discrimination legislations and laws.

Sian affirms: 'However despite these market-driven attempts to reimagine the traditional pub, as well as public order interventions around 'thug pubs'. The vast majority of pubs still continue to signify sites of exclusion in two key ways. Firstly, Many BME populations fear that they will experience forms of violent racism.' This proves that racism and discrimination is the on-going problem which will need a very strong and constant state intervention.

---

[26] Hsiao –Hung Pal and Benjamin Zephaniah,Angry White People.(Zed Books Limited .London.2016) Preview

L. Sood and V Sood (MD) proclaims: 'Why are African Americans at greater risk for COVID-19, as compared to other racial/ethnic groups? There are 3 possible explanations: (1) social determinants of health; (2) comorbidities and coexposures; and (3) genetic differences. Furthermore, why may rural African Americans be at even greater risk than urban African Americans? This health inequity is largely attributable to social determinants of health.'[27] It is their opinion that most African Americans are highly affected by the coved 19 virus because their poor living conditions, their exposure to high risk areas, and possibly because of their genetic mechanism of which I may agree with their first two opinions but I disagree with their opinion that African Americans 's genetic mechanism may be the cause.

Ferdinand(M.D), Batieste and Fleurestil(M.S) proclaim: 'The disparities in outcomes, which are largely attributable to a greater prevalence of comorbidities such as hypertension and obesity, in addition to adverse environmental and socioeconomic factors, highlight the necessity of specialized clinical approaches and programs for African Americans to address longstanding barriers to equitable care.'[28] This is confirms that living conditions and health conditions like obesity may be the cause for

---

[27] Lakshay Sood Vanita Sood (MD) (03 May 2020) (Being African American and Rural: A Double Jeopardy From COVID-19) The journal of Rural Health Online (Volume37, Issue1) (Pp 217-221) Available: https://doi.org/10.1111/jrh.12459 Accessed: 02/01/2021

[28] Keith Ferdinand(M.D).,Tivona Batieste and Mashl iFleurestil (M.S).(June 2020)(Contemporary and Future Concepts on Hypertension in African Americans: COVID-19 and Beyond. Journal of the National Medical Association. Online (Volume 112, Issue 3,) (Pages 315-323) Available:
https://doi.org/10.1016/j.jnma.2020.05.018 Accessed: 02/01/2021

high mortality in the African American community and not their genetic mechanism.

Holzer and Reaser affirms: 'Black applicants, especially less-educated black males, are also less likely to be hired at suburban establishments.'[29] This clearly proves that the black people especially the uneducated are not given equal opportunity as whites when it comes to job opportunities, housing and many more not because the black may be less qualified than the whites as most black people attend university education than the whites. Stearns , Nandan and Potochnick declare: 'Results include the presence of racially-specific effects of high school course of study, with racial/ethnic minority students in the middle course intensity ranges more likely to attend four-year college than Whites with similar coursework.'[30] This shows that the black students are forced to attend longer periods of study unlike the white students of the same qualification.

Taylor, Keeanga-Yamahtta proclaim: 'Racial discrimination, sanctioned by law in the South and custom and public policy in the North over much of the twentieth century, caused disparities between Blacks and whites in employment, poverty, housing quality, and access to education.'[31] This indicates that the USA social and

---

[29]Harry J.Holzera and JessReaser (Nov 200)(Black Applicants, Black Employees, and Urban Labor Market Policy) Journal of Urban Economics Online:(Volume 48, Issue 3,) (Pp 365-387) Available: https://doi.org/10.1006/juec.2000.2171 Accesed:02/01/2021

[30] Elizabeth Stearnsa ,Nandan Jhaa and Stephanie Potochnick (Race, secondary school course of study, and college type)May 2013 Social Science Research.Online (Volume 42, Issue 3) (Pages 789-803) Available: https://doi.org/10.1016/j.ssresearch.2013.01.007 Accessed:02/01/2021

[31]Taylor, Keeanga-Yamahtta. From #BlackLivesMatter to Black Liberation. (Chicago: Haymarket Books.2016)4

political system is set in a way that disadvantage the Black Americans and other ethnic minority in the areas of employment, housing and even education.

Reviewing the situation in the UK Good fellow asserts: 'Churchill's views on matters of race and migration were hardly abnormal. Before and after the 1955 election, politicians from the left and the right complained that people of colour coming to the UK would threaten the very idea of the nation and undermine Britons' standard of living by taking jobs and housing.'[32] This explains that it was not Churchill 's best interest to have black people in the UK as they had the mentality that black people would take jobs and housing which are meant for the Britons.

Goodfellow comments on Churchill: 'With the general election likely to happen within a year – one that would not, in the end , contest – he tried to persuade his colleagues to adopt a campaign slogan that was similar to the rallying cry of the far right in the decades that followed. ' Keep England white', he suggested, would be a good message.'[33] This is clear that Churchill did not want black people in the UK as he was of the idea to make England a white country only.

It is only when they wanted cover up the post-war worker shortages that they turned to the Caribbean Islands. This led to the Windrush generation. These are half a million people who came to the UK from the Caribbean between 1948 and 1971. These were

---

[32] Maya Goodfellow *Hostile Environment, How immigrants became scapegoats* (Veso Books. London.2019)50
[33] Maya Goodfellow *Hostile Environment, How immigrants became scapegoats.* 50

transported to the UK's shores with the aim of meeting post-war worker shortages. This generation was named after the name of the big ship in which they were transported which was called MV Empire Windrush. Through the 1971 Immigration Act some of them were later granted the indefinite leave to remain in the UK. It is a shame that most of them faced racism and inequality in the UK as they were not granted leave to remain in the UK legally. They had no documentation for them to be able to get jobs which makes them to be considered as illegal immigrants.

Goodfellow affirms: 'As well as the hostile environment, the obsession with numbers resulted in Operation Vaken which involved Theresa May's Home Office sending vans reading 'Go Home' around diverse parts of the country and boasting about immigration raids on social media.'[34] This indicates how the black people and other minority races who whore subjects to immigration lived in fear and hostile situations. The immigration crisis caused a lot of stress to the foreign nationals who loved in the UK of which some even took their own lives for fear of being deported to a country that no longer have anyone to return to.

Gentleman asserts: ' How do you pack for a one-way journey back to a country you left when you were eleven years and have not visited it for fifty years? Around lunch time on 24 October 2017, staff at the Yarl's Wood Immigration Removal centre in Bedfordshire told sixty-one year old Paulette Wilson to gather her belongings and get ready to be taken to another holding centre near Heathrow airport, where she was due to be placed on a

---

[34] Maya Goodfellow *Hostile Environment, How immigrants became scapegoats*.5

plane and sent back to Jamaica.'[35] This reflects the unfair situation in which the Windrush generation finds themselves in. It is clear that after fifty years in the country, UK had become Ms Wilson's home and she possibly had no one to return to in Jamaica. Considering the work that the Afro Caribbean people had done in the development of UK that include digging of the underground rail tunnels in London and around, It is not fair to deport them in such a disrespectful manner.

The Black lives movement

Yanco continues: 'The Kerner Commission was established by President Lyndon B. Johnson to investigate the causes of the uprisings that took place in cities across the country in the mid-1960s and to make recommendations for addressing the causes.'[36] This was a wise decision by President Johnson to try and alleviate the problems faced by the nation by reflecting on the effects of racism and inequality. 'It is good that Johnson acknowledged the existence of racism and he exposed it in order to eradicate it completely. It is pointless to trying to eradicate symptoms of the disease without treating the very disease causing symptoms.'[37] Yanco declares further: 'The commission pointed to white racism and persistent racial inequality as causes of the urban rebellions that had rocked major cities throughout the nation. Like Dr. King, the report's authors maintained that white America bore much of the responsibility.'[38] It was an accurate

---

[35] Amelia Gentleman. *The Windrush Betrayal.*(Bloomsbury House. London 2019)1-5

[36] Yanco, Jennifer J... Misremembering Dr. King : Revisiting the Legacy of Martin Luther King)54

[37] Emphasis: Mine

observation which the commission came out with to identify that the cause of the riots in US was due to racism and inequality. This is true of our world today which is evidenced by the formation of the black lives matter movement. If we are to solve the social problems we have to be bold enough to address the issues as Yanco recalls further outcome of the commission's investigation in February 1968: 'The report decried the neglect and isolation of African Americans in run-down, economically abandoned inner cities and recommended job creation, increased social services, diverse and better-trained police forces, and massive investments in decent housing.'[39] This speaks to our Postmodernity world that the solution to the problems of the riots and terrorism is in solving the issue of racism and inequality. This can be facilitated by the creation of better and fair social services, diverse and better-trained police forces, and large investments in decent and safe housing unlike the London Glenfell tower cladding that was the reason for the fires that killed more than seventy people in June 2017.

Meghan Markle and British racism

There are a lot of speculations about the inequality within the British royal family that might have led to Prince Harry and Merghan's decisions to live the royal family. Smith proclaims: 'Harry and Meghan's departure has prompted a nationwide reckoning about whether this former empire has made any significant progress tackling issues of racism and classism. The fight has been cast as the latest battle in a culture war dividing this country

---

[38] Yanco, Jennifer J... Misremembering Dr. King : Revisiting the Legacy of Martin Luther King)55
[39] Yanco, Jennifer J... Misremembering Dr. King : Revisiting the Legacy of Martin Luther King)55

and beyond.'[40] This highlight the need for the royal family to challenge and stop speculations on racism which may aim to divide the nations of the world. It could have sent a clear message of anti-discrimination to have her Majesty the queen of England publicly challenge any such speculations of inequality. Smith further draws from Ladapo: 'The collateral damage extends far beyond the palace walls. For Ladapo and others, Meghan's treatment has sent a damaging message to young British people of color, who perhaps saw her as a sign that racial prejudice might be finally ebbing away.

"This has been a very rude awakening," said Ladapo, who studies economics and is president of her university's African-Caribbean Society. "It reminded us that we shouldn't get too comfortable, and no matter how much we think we are accepted into society, we really aren't."'[41] This indicates that there is a great task to convince the black young generation that they are safe and accepted in the society. Since the Black Lives Matter demonstrations the UK government has made a lot of changes to indicate that inequality and discrimination is not acceptable in the UK. Many Television programmes appear to be including people of colour which helps the young people to feel more accepted within the British community. Intermarriages among the British population also send a clear message of anti-discrimination.

[40] Alexander Smith, Feb. 10, 2020, Article : (Meghan Markle and British racism)online : available: https://www.nbcnews.com/news/world/meghan-markle-british-racism-what-her-saga-says-black-britons-n1132181 Accessed: 27/09/2021

[41] Alexander Smith, Feb. 10, 2020, Article : (Meghan Markle and British racism)online : available: https://www.nbcnews.com/news/world/meghan-markle-british-racism-what-her-saga-says-black-britons-n1132181 Accessed: 27/09/2021

Spiggle affirms: 'Earlier this month, the world watched Oprah's much-talked-about interview with Prince Harry and Meghan Markle (Markle). There were a lot of eye-opening things said during that interview, especially by Markle.

One of the two most notable points concerned the racism Markle faced when becoming part of the British royal family. The other had to do with the mental health struggles she endured, including difficulty in obtaining mental health help.

Dealing with racism or suicidal thoughts, while extremely unfortunate, are hardly new challenges for many people. But what was so surprising was that someone as influential, powerful and connected as Markle would not only have to face these things, but have so much trouble getting the help she needed.'[42] This shows that discrimination have a great impact on the mental wellbeing. There is a great need to offer a listening ear to those who suffer abuse before their mental health is affected. At times it is pride that stands on the ways for famous people to open up about the challenges they face. Had it been that Markle and Harry opened up in time, they could have been helped before making their final decision to move out of the royal family. Friel and Hosie draws from the words of Harry in his interview with Oprah 'Harry said racism was "a large part" of why the couple left the UK, they claim a member of the royal family raised "concerns" over how dark Archie's skin would be before he was born, and Markle said her treatment in the tabloids compared to that of Kate Middleton was racist.'[43]

---

[42] Tom Spiggle, Mar 23, 2021,(What Meghan Markle's Experiences Tell Us About Mental Health And Racism At Work.)Online . Available: https://www.forbes.com/sites/tomspiggle/2021/03/23/what-meghan-markles-experiences-tell-us-about-mental-health-and-racism-at-work/?sh=12f67d083fa3 Accessed: 27/09/2021

This may mean that Harry and Meghan may be angry and regretting that they left the royal family. At times people may ask certain questions or say things unaware and end up being misunderstood which may be the case with questions about the skin colour of Archie.

Inequality in Zimbabwe

Matikiti proclaims: ' Racism was a major threat to community-building in post-colonial Zimbabwe. One characteristic of white settlement in Rhodesia that continued in the new Zimbabwe was that the white community kept itself largely separate from the black and Asian communities in the country. Urban white people lived in separate areas of town, and white people had their own segregated education, healthcare and recreational facilities. Marriage between black and white people was possible, but remains to the present day very rare but remains uncommon.'[44]This indicates the difficulties of tribalism and racism in Zimbabwe where intermarriages are still rare. On the other perspective the other race may feel superior to the other for them to intermarry. Yet custom and tradition may be a hindrance to intermarriage. Independence marked unity and solidarity of the oppressed people against a racist and oppressive political

---

[43] Mikhaila Friel and Rachel Hosie Insider. Mar 10, 2021, (The British royal family has turned a blind eye to its racist past) Online article. Available: https://www.insider.com/british-royal-family-racist-history-black-lives-matter-2020-8 Accessed: 27/09/2021

[44] Taylor and Francis Group. (Politics and Religion in Zimbabwe.) Online article: available: https://www.taylorfrancis.com/chapters/edit/10.4324/9780367823993-12/robert-gabriel-mugabe-black-african-theologian-philosopher-robert-matikiti accessed: 27/09/2021

order established through the institutions of colonialism. The song encouraged and motivated the white racists in the midst of uncertainties. There has to be a way of getting together and equally sharing our natural resources. Mutondi highlights on the Zimbabwe land reform program which originally aimed at promoting equality and diversity: 'The model aims to empower black entrepreneurs through access to land and inputs and to close the gap between the white and black commercial farmers.'[45] After the independence of Zimbabwe from the white colonial rule, the new government ventured into the land reform programme with the aim of equally sharing the land and natural resources in Zimbabwe but it was unfortunate that Mugabe ended up taking all the land from the whites without a proper sharing and negotiations. Had it been dealt with properly, Zimbabwe could have been one of the prosperous countries in Africa (the bread basket of Africa).

Moyo, Sam, Chambati and Walter, affirm: 'Land reform was meant to redress historical settler-colonial land dispossession and the related racial and foreign domination, as well as the class-based agrarian inequalities which minority rule promoted.'[46] This elaborates the good intensions behind the Zimbabwe land reform programme which was meant to promote equality and diversity although it all went wrong along the way as the new government became under the influence of racism and hatred for the white people. Moyo, Sam, Chambati and Walter draws from Vudzijena: 'Instead, the whole

---

[45] Matondi, Prosper B... *Zimbabwe's Fast Track Land Reform.*(London: Zed Books. 2012)xi

[46] Moyo, Sam, and Chambati, Walter, eds. (Land and Agrarian Reform in Zimbabwe : Beyond White-Settler Capitalism. Dakar: Codesria 2013)30

land reform was deemed a 'chaotic and often violent', 'racially motivated land seizure' and 'politically vindictive land grab', which violated the legitimate land rights of white farmers (see Willems 2005). Putatively, the FTLRP only benefited President Mugabe's cronies and destroyed agriculture (Bond 2005), while the statutory land user rights provided to the beneficiaries by the state are allegedly insecure, leading to ubiquitous land disputes (Vudzijena 2007).'[47] Although the black Zimbabweans had the right to equal distribution of the land, the motive behind land grabbing was not right as it was violent, racially motivated and politically malicious. All the land was forcefully taken away from the white farmers and unlawfully distributed to the Zimbabwean war veterans who did not have farming tools and skills which led to the downfall of the economy of Zimbabwe which was held by farming. Moyo, Sam, Chambati and Walter goes on asserting: 'The first phase of the FTLRP was dominated by extensive popular and 'illegal' land occupations and the mass designation of over 3,000 farm properties for expropriation.'[48] This shows how war veterans lawlessly and disorderly grabbed land and properties from white farmers. This act was inhuman and unacceptable and it should have been condemned by the government but their silence indicated that the government supported this behaviour which continued to destroy the Zimbabwean economy and their relationship with Europe and America.

The Apostle Paul declares: Gal. 3:27 – 28 (NRSV) 'As many of you were baptized into Christ have clothed yourselves with Christ. There is no longer Jew or Greek,

---

[47] Moyo, Sam, Chambati and Walter, eds. (*Land and Agrarian Reform in Zimbabwe*)32 ,33

[48] Moyo, Sam, Chambati and Walter, eds. (Land and Agrarian Reform in Zimbabwe)35

there is no longer slave or free, there is no longer male or female; for all of you are one in Christ Jesus'[49] This may indicate that Paul might have noticed discrimination in the Christian community which he was addressing. Ruben affirms further : 'Today's church, while recognizing that questions of ethnic identity in the ancient world differ greatly from modern conceptions of race, embraces Paul's eschatological vision of a community in which distinctions of race, class, and gender are transcended in Christ as a normative statement for understanding Christian identity.'[50] This may indicate that through civilization and education in the modern church racism my not be a big problem as it used to be in the past although we still face these challenges.

Medieval and pre- modern prejudices

Ruben draws from the social historians : 'Within academic discourse there exists a consensus opinion that the Industrial Revolution and the growth of capitalism are directly responsible for the rise of American racist thought'[51] Attributing racism to Modernism may appear as a way of justifying it no wonder why this ideology is challenged by modern scholars: 'Historian James H. Sweet argues that the identification of blackness with servitude characteristic of American racism was part of the western European cultural matrix long before the discovery of the New World and the rise of the Atlantic slave trade.'[52] This means that racism may also be

---

[49] Gal 3:27-28
[50] Rosario Rodriguez, Ruben.*Racism and God-Talk: A Latino/a Perspective.*(NYU Press, 2008)1

[51]Rosario Rodriguez, Ruben *Racism and God-Talk: A Latino/a Perspective.*)3,4

attributed to the western European cultural matrix in the history of Abraham with the Hebrew nation. It could be a serious misinterpretation of theology to justify inequality based how God dealt with the Hebrew nation and other nations as human understanding of the ways of God may be limited and therefore unqualified to question the acts of the creator.

Ruben declares: 'Medieval and pre-modern prejudices traceable to Jewish, Christian, and Muslim attitudes about ethnic and religious otherness gave rise to the notion of European cultural superiority that eventually manifested itself as racial prejudice based on skin color. At some point in each of their histories, all three Abrahamic faiths have espoused the view that sub-Saharan Africans were culturally inferior and therefore naturally suited for slavery, yet few studies have explicitly examined how the confessional commitments of these faith traditions might contribute to — or counter — a racist worldview'[53] This explains how racism was based on the skin colour in which sub-Saharan Africans were considered as being inferior and suitable for slavery.

Racism in America

The horrendous killing of George Floyd by a Police man in United States moved from just being a local incident to a global protest against racial inequality and injustice. Since that incident, there has been a worldwide response with around two thousand gatherings and protests worldwide. The black lives matter movement took

---

[52]Rosario Rodriguez, Ruben *Racism and God-Talk: A Latino/a Perspective.*)3
[53]Rosario Rodriguez, Ruben Racism and God-Talk: A Latino/a Perspective.)4

it to the streets of UK in protest of the brutal killing of George Floyd by the US police officer who knelt on his throat until he passed out. Because of the uniform problems of racism and inequality in the UK ,the Black lives matter protesters went on to pulling down and drowning the stature of Edward Colstun who was an English merchant, slave trader, philanthropist and Tory Member of Parliament in the 17th century.

Drawing from the works of Tribble and Valerie: 'Leaders in diverse religious contexts are urged to consider the compounded systems of injustice that exacerbated the public protests in the present era, which I refer as "Black Lives Matter times," to distinguish the macro- level societal dynamics from the responses of resistant protest movements discussed throughout the book.'[54] Tribble and Valarie are advising the government to quickly respond to injustice as soon as it is noticed rather than waiting until it the world takes it to their hands in protests. Of which true that the oppressed people also do have a breaking point when they can no longer take any more from their oppressors but to fight to justice. Asserting further Tribble and Valerie declare: 'Foremost for reader clarity, these assertions about ecclesial dilemmas of theoethical engagement in public witness must not be construed as an urban black existential problem that solely requires a black church response. Rather the shared responsibility for justice in this era of Black Lives matter times requires interreligious and ecumenical faith communities , including self –identified evangelical churches across the nation, to work collaboratively to address injustices.'[55] This means that it

---

[54] Milles Tribble and Valerie A. *Change Agent Church in Black Lives Matter Times:Urgency* Fortress Academic 2020)7
[55] Milles Tribble and Valerie A. *Change Agent Church in Black Lives*

must not be left for a few individuals to fight against the inequality and injustices but for the entire world to join together as a team to stop this.

Elaborating on the inequality with the USA judiciary system, Taylor, Keeanga-Yamahtta assert: 'The entire criminal justice system operates at the expense of African American communities and society as a whole. This crisis goes beyond high incarceration rates; indeed, the perpetuation of deeply ingrained stereotypes of African Americans as particularly dangerous, impervious to pain and souring, careless and carefree, and exempt from empathy, solidarity, or basic humanity is what allows the police to kill Black people with no threat of punishment.'[56] This explains how the USA judiciary system doesn't promote equality or protect the Black Americans instead the USA Judiciary system may be facilitating the incarceration making the black Americans vulnerable. The unchecked police brutality and murder evidences Taylor, Keeanga-Yamahtta's point of view that the judiciary may be behind all this. This does not mean that the Black Americans are always right as evidences Taylor, Keeanga-Yamahtta goes on asserting that : 'At the same time, Black poverty, imprisonment, and premature death are widely seen as the products of Black insolence and lapsed personal responsibility.'[57] This may suggest that at times the black Americans may be the cause of this animosity between them and the police by being violent but this is not always the case. Yanco proclaims : 'Few have bothered to look at institutionally backed white

---

Matter Times:Urgency,8
[56] Taylor, Keeanga-Yamahtta. *From #BlackLivesMatter to Black Liberation*. (Chicago: Haymarket Books.2016)3
[57] Taylor, Keeanga-Yamahtta. *From #BlackLivesMatter to Black Liberation*. (Chicago: Haymarket Books.2016)6

culture and the role it has played in creating and fuelling problems in the African American community.'[58] This calls for us to reflect on the issues in the white culture that may not be acceptable in the black America communities.

Reflecting on the violence which was started by Donald Trump supporters in US on the 07/01//2021 as reported from online Telegraph , Smith, Sabur and Allen asserts: 'Five dead in US Capitol riot after Donald Trump's supporters storm Washington - everything we know : In chaotic scenes in Washington DC, protesters stormed their way into the heart of American democracy'[59] This is an indication that even white people do some violent demonstrations but these cases are not equally treated by the state compared to the cases that involves the black Americans. According to New York times Trump stirred up violence after he had lost elections. Marovich asserts: "Trump Told Crowd 'You Will Never Take Back Our Country With Weakness''[60] Although Trump may be misinterpreted, It appears as if as Congress prepared to certify the victory of his successor, President Trump railed against the election and helped set in motion hours of violence. This is obvious that the President of US

---

[58] Yanco, Jennifer J... Misremembering Dr. King : Revisiting the Legacy of Martin Luther King)54

[59] Ben Riley-Smith, Rozina Sabur and Nick Allen. (8 January 2021) Five dead in US Capitol riot after Donald Trump's supporters storm Washington) USA, (US Election, US Politics, Donald Trump The telegraph, Online, available :
https://www.telegraph.co.uk/news/2021/01/08/us-capitol-riot-protest-what-happened-who-died-trump-supporters/ Accessed :08/01/21

[60] Pete Marovich (06/01/21) (The Presidential Transition)The New York Times Online . Available:
https://www.nytimes.com/2021/01/06/us/politics/trump-speech-capitol.html Accessed: 08/01/21

was behind the violence in the US as his speech motivated his supported to use violence in order to take power back. The black lives matter did not storm the capital as did Trump protesters yet the police and the military dealt severely and brutally with the black lives matter protestors.

Sean asserts: 'On August 9, 2014, Darren Wilson of the Ferguson, Missouri, Police Department (FPD) shot and killed Michael Brown, an eighteen-year-old African American man and recent high school graduate. Wilson fired twelve shots, at least six of which hit Brown, who was unarmed. The most serious crime of which Michael Brown was suspected at the time of his death was the theft of a box of cigarillos from a nearby convenience store. 1 In grand jury testimony, Wilson defended his use of deadly force, testifying that while the two men struggled, Brown "had the most intense aggressive face. The only way I can describe it, it looks like a demon ." Wilson, who never faced criminal charges for the killing, went on to assert that the teenaged Brown "looked like he was almost bulking up to run through the shots, like it was making him mad that I'm shooting at him."'[61] This proves that the police officer was very proud that he shot and killed Brown. I wonder how the judge was convinced by Mr Wilson's justification of his behaviour which based on hatred and racism of which this shows how the USA judiciary system worked in favour of the white people. Still on the same incident Malloy affirms further: 'An investigation of the FPD by the U.S. Department of Justice (DOJ) in the months that followed determined that Wilson's behaviour was far from an isolated incident. The

---

[61] Sean Malloy, L. *Out of Oakland : Black Panther Party Internationalism during the Cold War.* Ithaca: Cornell University Press. 2017)241

DOJ "found substantial evidence of racial bias among police and court staff in Ferguson," concluding that "he harms of Ferguson's police and court practices are borne disproportionately by African Americans, and there is evidence that this is due in part to intentional discrimination on the basis of race."'[62] It was proved that the U.S. police worked under the influence of hatred and racism. The question of injustice still remains as there were no further charges against USA police instead following Mr Brown's death protesters were met with the USA military together with the armed police response. Oh what horrible and terrible situation racism brings to the U.S. communities?

Gini and Green proclaim: 'The concept of courage is usually associated with physical acts of derring-do that involve danger, risk, and behaviour. Abraham Lincoln and Rosa Parks, two people who lived decades apart and who stood on opposite sides of America's racial divide, nevertheless both exemplify courage, and remain classic examples of physical and moral courage. Just as Abraham Lincoln deserves to be remembered for preserving the Union and for helping to eradicate the "sin of slavery," so too Rosa Parks deserves to be remembered as the "mother of the Civil Rights Movement." Each of these individuals had different talents and temperaments and they faced different kinds of challenges, in different circumstances, and in different times.'[63] This tells us that we can change

---

[62] Sean Malloy, L. Out of Oakland : Black Panther Party Internationalism during the Cold War. Ithaca: Cornell University Press. 2017)241

[63] Al Gini Ronald M. Green. (25 March 2013) Abraham Lincoln/Rosa Parks: Moral.Wiley online library Available: https://doi-org.dtl.idm.oclc.org/10.1002/9781118551653.ch7 Accessed: 10/01/2021

the situation of racism and inequality without putting our lives on the line to risk. It took courage and determination for Rosa Parks to challenge the racism and inequality as she refused changed the way things were that black people should sit at the back of the bus and to give their seats to white people if they needed them. Theoharis asserts: 'Parks wrote of "poverty, segregation, threats" of her youth, along with the spirit of resistance and self-respect inculcated by her grandfather and mother.'[64] This indicates that Parks' grandparents laid a very strong foundation of hatred for racism and inequality which Parks later had to challenge and change. This generation needs parents who will confidently ground their children in the right and well-mannered culture that embraces all people equally regardless of race.

President Abraham Lincoln is remembered for helping to stop slavery in America. Fredrickson asserts: 'Respect for Lincoln and his legacy among African Americans reflected the mood of optimism about the achievement of racial equality and fraternity that prevailed in the early 1960s, culminating in the Civil Rights Acts of 1964 and 1965.'[65] This means that Lincoln will always be remembered for the achievement of racial equality in America and the entire world. Lincoln did not easily achieve his breakthrough on the abolition of slavery as he had risk his own life and later died for his decisions to advocate the freedom of the black Americans.

---

[64] Jeanne Theoharis, *The Rebellious Life of Mrs. Rosa Parks* (Beacon Press Massachusetts 2013)x

[65] Fredrickson, George M., and Fredrickson, George M..*Big Enough to Be Inconsistent : Abraham Lincoln Confronts Slavery and Race.* Cambridge: Harvard University Press.2008)18

Malcom X is also remembered for being a popular figure during the civil rights movement as he risked his own life to advocate for the equal rights of the African Americans and the Nation of Islam in America. Malcom X advocated for black self-defense, and black economic autonomy, black power and cheered racial pride. Mostern draws from X who asserted that : 'if the forces of law prove unable, or inadequate, or reluctant to protect those white from those Negroes – then those white people should protect and defend themselves from those Negroes, using arms if necessary. And I feel that when the law fails to protect Negroes from whites' attack, then those Negroes should use arms, if necessary, to defend themselves.'"[66] It looks like Malcom was encouraging the use of violence to bring about a change. I disagree with him in that this ideology is ungodly as the scripture tells us that vindication belongs to God. It is obvious that X 's principles were grounded on the Quran which is very different from the Holy Scriptures I believe in. We cannot correct the wrong with the wrong. It is like trying to extinguish fire by pouring fuel on the burning fire.

Discussing equality in diversity we cannot forget about Ella Josephine Baker an African-American civil rights and human rights advocate. Baker is remembered for her key role in some of the most significant organizations of the period, including the NAACP and the Student Nonviolent Coordinating Committee. She is also remembered for challenging school policies that she thought were unfair as a student. Gillespie draws from Baker: "'We on the outside want to be important, so we ape the insiders,' she asserted, and, in so doing, replicate

---

[66] Kenneth Mostern . *Autobiography and Black Identity Politics : Racialization in Twentieth-Century* America. Cambridge: Cambridge University Press.1999)149

the hierarchies of inequality.'[67] Baker appeared to challenge the life of compromise and mediocre that follows the systems of racism and inequality that had been put in place by their predecessors.

We cannot look at the lives of those that brought a change without mentioning Vaclav Havel who was the founder of the Civic Forum a political party in that challenged communism in Czech as they protested against violence. Although he came from a wealthy and a well-educated family he laid down his life for many and was often arrested and serving prison sentence. Cohen assert: 'He argued for rewarding personal responsibility over party loyalty and insisted that the Communist Party could be reformed only if there were sufficient outside pressure— a need to compete with an opposition party for popular support. A two-party system, with both parties committed to democratic socialism, was, he insisted, essential.'[68] This illustrates Havel's boldness and sacrifice to confront dangerous communists who were well known for their brutality and mercilessness.

Angela Yvonne Davis is also remembered for being an American political activist, philosopher, academic, and author who an American political activist, philosopher, academic, and author and a Black Panther who challenged Police brutality in the 1970s. Zamalin elaborates Davis's opinion on abolition: 'Racial disparity defines contemporary American mass incarceration. According to one influential sociological interpretation, the prison is the

---

[67] Michele Gillespie, and McMillen, Sally G., eds. *North Carolina Women : Their Lives and Times, Volume 2.* Athens: University of Georgia Press.2015)263

[68]Cohen, Warren I. *Profiles in Humanity : The Battle for Peace, Freedom, Equality, and Human Rights.*)27.

most recent instalment of a history of racial oppression, what the sociologist Loïc Wacquant calls the fourth "peculiar" race-based American institution of social control that first began with chattel slavery before continuing through Jim Crow and then the black ghetto'[69] This highlight the fact that prisons have become a tool that facilitates racism. It appears as if most black people are targeted for incarceration unlike the white folks. A minor offense easily lead to a prison sentence for black people not that they are the most offenders. It looks like Police uses stereotype and prejudice to generalise that blacks are the most offenders. Black people are most associated with drugs and theft which is very wrong as most blacks are law abiding.

When it comes to non-violent struggle for democracy and human rights, a Burmese politician, diplomat, author, and a 1991 Nobel Peace Prize laureate Aung San Suu Kyi is remembered. Suu Kyi is known for her leadership skills in the National League for Democracy in Burma. It is her boldness and sacrifice to stand up for democracy which made her very popular in the world. Kane proclaims: 'Suu Kyi had publicly committed herself to Burma ' s '' second struggle '' and taken her W rst step on a rapid climb to the e V ective leadership of the democratic forces.'[70] This evidences the fact that Suu Kyi was brave to challenge his nation and to take rise up to the position of the president which could have cost her life as it did with her own father. This is a challenge to everyone to stand up for what is right despite risks.

---

[69] Zamalin, Alex. *Struggle on Their Minds : The Political Thought of African American Resistance.* New York: Columbia University Press.2017)120

[70] Kane, John. *The Politics of Moral Capital.* (Cambridge: Cambridge University Press.2001)149

Jack Greenberg a Jewish American attorney and legal scholar who was well known for being the Director-Counsel of the NAACP Legal Defence Fund a leading United States civil rights organization and law firm based in New York City from 1961 to 1984. Greenberg was well-known for being the only white legal counsellor for the NAACP Legal Defence and Educational Fund. This was a great sacrifice for him to choose to suffer with the minority just as Moses in Genesis chose to be identified with the Hebrews rather than to enjoy the comfort of the Egyptian palace. Cohen refers to Greenberg's commitment and determination to stand for civil rights: 'When Greenberg saw his FBI file years later, he discovered that the agency was aware of a plot by white racists to assassinate him, but never bothered to warn him. None of the threats to his life seem to have intimidated him.'[71] This shows that by choosing to challenge the nation for racism and inequality Greenberg had put his own life danger as the white people had a plot to assassinate him. In order to make a difference it takes a great sacrifice.

Inequality and racism in South Africa

The history of inequality and discrimination in South Africa goes back even to the pre- colonial era during the time of Shaka the Zulu and the Mzilikazi and the Ndebele. Ndlovu affirms: 'The phenomenon of "black-on-black" violence among the people of Africa has, ever since the

---

[71] Cohen, Warren I.(*Profiles in Humanity : The Battle for Peace, Freedom, Equality, and Human Rights*. Lanham, MD: Rowman & Littlefield Publishers 2009)91

advent of modernity/coloniality, been articulated in such a way that it presents victims as perpetrators. Thus, from the *Mfecane* violence of the "pre-colonial" era to the xenophobic/Afrophobic violence of the "post-colonial" era in Africa, incidents of black-on-black violence have always attracted explanations that cast doubt on the humanity of the black subject, through the colonial strategy of inventing and inverting causation. This colonial strategy entails both mis-presenting the epochal history of coloniality by representing it in terms of rupture instead of continuity, as well as representing the indigenous African subject as inherently violent. I argue in this article that black-on-black violence is a product of coloniality—a racist global power structure that makes incidents of "non-revolutionary violence" among the oppressed black subject inevitable. Thus, I deploy the case of the *Mfecane* violence of the "pre-colonial" era in southern Africa, and the Afro-phobic attacks on foreign nationals in "post-apartheid" South Africa to unmask the *longue durée* of coloniality, and its role of manufacturing blackon-black violence among the black people of Africa.'[72] This explains how there were tribal wars within the black people of South Africa long before they were colonised by the white people. There other tribe claimed superiority over the other and only the superior tribe was allowed to choose the bride from the other tribes within the same nation. This led to the migration (Umfecane) as Mzilikazi was in opposition of this

---

[72] Morgan Ndlovu (2017) Manufacturing Black-on-Black Violence in Africa: A Decolonial Perspective on Mfecane and Afrophobia/Xenophobia in South Africa, International Journal of African Renaissance Studies - Multi-, Inter- and Transdisciplinarity, 12:2, 97-109, DOI: 10.1080/18186874.2017.1401768. Accessed: 27/09/2021

ideology therefore creating animosity with Tshaka.(Shaka).

With Mzilikazi running away from Tshaka and settling in the now Zimbabwe forming a tribe of the Ndebele which again cause long lasting tensions between the Shona and the Ndebele people.

In December 1956 Nelson Mandela and the other 155 members of the ANC were accused of high treason (Trying to overthrow the state)and arrested just because they advocated equality for the black South African people. Referring to Mandela Warren asserts: 'In a speech that his biographer Anthony Sampson called the most effective of his career, he spoke of his ideals, of the democratic state of which he dreamed, of a multiracial nation in which no one would be discriminated against because of colour or ethnicity, in which opportunity for all would be equal. He stood before the court as the representative, indeed the leader, of all opponents of apartheid.'[73] This shows that Mandela was determined to sacrifice his own freedom in order to liberate his fellow black South Africans from the White colonial oppression and apartheid. He considered and supported diversity within the population of South Africa. Mandela was willing to embrace other tribes and nationalities that had made South Africa their own home and he was willing share residence with all people without discrimination. It is a shame that this changed after Mandela's death as South Africans became xenophobic brutally killing by burning other foreigners in South Africa.

Crush, Jonathan, Chikanda, Abel, Skinner and Caroline asserts: 'The common perception that migrants

---

[73] Cohen, Warren I. *Profiles in Humanity : The Battle for Peace, Freedom, Equality, and Human Rights.* (Lanham, MD: Rowman & Littlefield Publishers.2009)134

are far more successful entrepreneurs than South Africans in the informal economy has prompted a new focus on migrant entrepreneurial motivation and comparisons with South African entrepreneurship'[74] This indicates that the local South Africans were becoming jealousy that businesses owned by the Immigrants appeared to be flourishing. From my own experience in South Africa I found out that Foreigners in South Africa were hard working compared to local South Africans who appeared to be pursuing homemade African beer known as

(Umqombothi) instead of pursuing education and employment. Jealousy could also be another source of racism in the US where the black Americans seem to be prospering with an example of Obama as the first African American president.

Yanco goes on drawing from King: 'While Dr. King focused much of his attention on the United States, he was well aware that racism was a global problem. "Racism," he said, "is no mere American phenomenon. Its vicious grasp knows no geographical boundaries. In fact, racism and its perennial ally— economic exploitation— provide the key to understanding most of the international complications of this generation."[75] This proves that racism is a global phenomenon where Africans are found discriminating against other Africans of different tribes.

Crush, Jonathan, Chikanda, Abel, and Skinner, Caroline further affirm: 'Furthermore, nearly 60 per cent felt that reasons for the xenophobic violence of 2008

---

[74] Crush, Jonathan, Chikanda, Abel, and Skinner, Caroline, eds. *Mean Streets : Migration, Xenophobia and Informality in South Africa. Cape Town:* (Southern African Migration Programme (SAMP)2015)5.
[75] Yanco, Jennifer J... Misremembering Dr. King : Revisiting the Legacy of Martin Luther King Jr.)52

included that migrants take jobs from South Africans and that they do not belong in the country.'[76] This is indication that foreigners in South Africa were hard working as they pursued employment. It is obvious that any employer would prefer hard working employees rather than someone who only hang around only to get the pay for the job they did not do as Crush, Jonathan, Chikanda, Abel, and Skinner, Caroline proclaim: 'At the same time, only 16 per cent of South Africans claimed that they had personally been denied a job because it was given to a foreign national.'[77] This is a proof that employers preferred to employ foreign nationals for the reason of their hard work.

It only takes the strong measures from the judiciary system to promote equality in such a diverse population like US and South Africa unless the government is behind such violence to promote it as Crush, Jonathan, Chikanda, Abel, and Skinner, Caroline further declare: '.. the violence will not stop until there are robust sanctions against perpetrators through hate crime legislation and other measures, criminal charges are laid and convictions secured. This is a matter of the South African state respecting basic human rights. This needs to be combined with much stronger statements from national and local leaders, politicians and bureaucrats condemning violence perpetrated against migrants. The claims of police complicity need to be investigated and firmly dealt with.'[78]

---

[76]Crush, Jonathan, Chikanda, Abel, and Skinner, Caroline,(eds). *Mean Streets : Migration, Xenophobia and Informality in South Africa.*)5.
[77] Crush, Jonathan, Chikanda, Abel, and Skinner, Caroline,(eds). Mean Streets : Migration, Xenophobia and Informality in South Africa.)7.
[78] Crush, Jonathan, Chikanda, Abel, and Skinner, Caroline,(eds). Mean Streets : Migration, Xenophobia and Informality in South Africa.)18

This may indicate that the government may be guilty breaching human rights as they by not taking draconian measures against such perpetrators through hate crime legislation and laying criminal charges on them. This makes me to reflect own how the US president showed a cold shoulder at the brutality killing of George Floyd. Schultheis draws from the works of Wiesel : ' I swore never to be silent whenever and wherever human beings endure suffering and humiliation. We must always take sides. Neutrality helps the oppressor, never the victim. Silence encourages the tormentor, never the tormented.'[79] This explains that it is the responsibility of the state to take action to stop the bad behaviour rather than being quiet about it as their quietness may be an indication that they may be in favour of the behaviour.

Crush, Jonathan, Chikanda, Abel, and Skinner, Caroline continue to proclaim: 'What makes the official position especially ironic is when officials themselves articulate sentiments that reproduce the xenophobic myths that they claim do not exist. A senior official in the Department of Home Affairs, for example, is reported to have informed South African MPs that "if you go to Alexandra, you go to Sunnyside, you go everywhere, spaza shops, hair salons, everything has been taken over by foreign nationals…they displace South Africans by making them not competitive" (van der Westhuizen, 2011). At an official meeting, then National Police Commissioner Bheki Cele characterized immigrants and refugees as "people who jump borders," were flooding into the country and destroying the livelihoods of South

---

[79] Michael J. Schultheis(1989)(Journal Refugees in Africa: The Geopolitics of Forced Displacement) African Studies Review (Online) (Vol. 32, No. 1) (Pp. 3-29) Available: https://www.jstor.org/stable/524491 Accessed : 04/01/21

African informal traders.'⁸⁰ This clearly demonstrate that the government of South Africa could engineering the violence against the foreign nationals in South Africa as this resulted to many foreign nationals being beaten and some burned to death by the local South African who felt motivated to carry put order which had been done by the foreign nationals. Some of the violence against the foreign nationals was uploaded on YouTube where rocks and bricks were used to crash the head of foreign nationals. Some foreign nationals were repeatedly beated on the head with stick to their death : (https://www.youtube.com/watch?v=ma73FHuut5k)

Neocosmos declares: 'It is apparent then that an authoritarian culture permeates all repressive apparatuses of the state, and that this authoritarianism is directed particularly towards noncitizens of African origin.'⁸¹ This again proves that the South African government supported the killing of the foreign nationals within South Africa . It is a shame that instead of promoting equality in the diversity of the population of South Africa the government had the blood of these innocent people on their own hands as Neocosmos continues to confirm that: 'The Zimbabwe Herald referred to NGO sources to suggest that three Zimbabweans a month die at Lindela and are buried in paupers' graves (Herald , 25 January 2005). In October 2004, the Mozambican consul-general was quoted as saying that 'so far 20 Mozambicans held at Lindela have died for unexplained causes (sic)' (Business Day , 12

---

[80] Crush, Jonathan, Chikanda, Abel, and Skinner, Caroline,(eds). Mean Streets : Migration, Xenophobia and Informality in South Africa.)49

[81] Neocosmos, Michael. *From Foreign Natives to Native Foreigners : Explaining Xenophobia in Post-Apartheid South Africa.* Dakar: CODESRIA 2010)

October 2004).'[82] This indicates that this ruthless massacre of foreign nationals was public as it was published on the newspapers yet the government did not challenge it. It is not only black that were targeted by tribalism in South Africa as Durrheim affirms: 'Increasing numbers of rural whites had become landless, with 17.5 per cent of white families living in 'great poverty' and beginning to integrate with black communities (Iliffe 1988). They either did menial work on farms (usually alongside black workers) for meagre wages or they moved to towns to live in multiracial slums such as Sophiatown or Alexandra near Johannesburg.'[83] This means that many white land owners had their land taken from them bringing them into poverty in their own country of birth. To make matters even worse in 2018 many white farmers were beaten to death during the early hours of the morning by the black rioting groups with the example of my classmate Sharon whose father was brutally beaten and left for death for being white in South Africa. From the University of the West of Scotland, Sharon suspended her classes and flew back to South Africa to take care of her agonising father.

We cannot help but think of the situation in US during the times of Martin Luther King Junior as Finley, Lou, LaFayette, Bernard, Jr., Ralph , Smith and Pam draws from Daley: 'We were not free to move into the southern or northern suburbs. You had a segregated city, unlike some other cities, with African Americans on this side, Irish and Polish on that side, the Jewish community

---

[82]Neocosmos, Michael. *From Foreign Natives to Native Foreigners : Explaining Xenophobia in Post-Apartheid South Africa*. Dakar: CODESRIA 2010)94

[83] Kevin Durrheim. *Race Trouble : Race, Identity and Inequality in Post-Apartheid South Africa*. (Lanham, MD: Lexington Books. 2011)9

living on the Near North Side, and a big-time, centralized, powerful mayor who was anti-progressive at the time'[84] It is clear that racism existed in US from long time ago where ethnic minority publicly suffered from discrimination from the US government. Yanco goes on asserting 'This "special treatment" began when Africans were first brought to this country in chains and has continued in various forms up into the present. This has entailed receiving second-class education; being excluded from voting and civic participation and from large sectors of the job market; having limited access to public facilities such as hospitals, transportation, and recreational facilities; being banned from white neighbourhoods and entire towns; being refused FHA loans, the benefits of the GI Bill, farm loans, and extension services; being subject to unethical scientific experimentation such as the infamous Tuskegee syphilis study; being excluded from hotels, restaurants, and other commercial spaces; being incarcerated at much higher rates than whites; and being subject to white terrorism and murdered with impunity—individually in the case of lynching, or as whole communities as in the case of 1921 Greenwood massacre in Tulsa, Oklahoma.'[85] This proves that racism is not a new thing but it existed even in the introduction of slavery when the whites turned to Africa for free labour.

Cohen reflects on Gandhi's reaction to racism and inequality in South Africa: 'Gandhi discovered that in the Afrikaner-controlled Orange Free State, Indians were by

---

[84] Finley, Mary Lou, LaFayette, Bernard, Jr., Ralph, James R., Jr., and Smith, Pam, eds. *The Chicago Freedom Movement : Martin Luther King Jr. and Civil Rights Activism in the North.* Lexington: University Press of Kentucky.2016)237

[85] Yanco, Jennifer J... Misremembering Dr. King : Revisiting the Legacy of Martin Luther King Jr.)53

law denied virtually all rights. They could remain in the territory only as menials. In Transvaal, also Afrikaner-controlled, they could neither vote nor own property. They were charged a poll tax for entering. They were not allowed outdoors after 9 p.m. without a permit.'[86] This shows how the Indians suffered discrimination during the South African apartheid where they were denied all rights. Gandhi was very brave to condemn racism against his fellow Indians who lived in South Africa. After the black South Africans were liberated from the apartheid regime they also inherited hatred and racism which was practised on foreign nationals in South Africa who were burned to death using the old car tyres.

In South Africa there was Donald James Woods who was a South African anti-apartheid activist and a journalist. He was a friend of an activist called Steve Biko, who detained and killed by the South African police. Donald sought for refuge in Lesotho for fear of his own life.Drawing from the words of Woods, Reid asserts: 'Woods advises that for the most part, there is nothing in the national life of South Africans above the master/servant relationship that encourages contact or friendship between Black and White (1988).'[87] This indicates that Woods identified racism that the black people suffered where they were not legally allowed to relate with the white people except for work relations

[86] Warren Cohen I.. *Profiles in Humanity : The Battle for Peace, Freedom, Equality, and Human Rights.* Lanham, MD: Rowman & Littlefield Publishers. 2009.)7

[87] Merlene V. Reid . .(2014) (Perspective Transformation Theory and the Donald Woods Experience From Racist to Anti-Apartheid Activist). Prejudice Reduction and Transformation theory (OnlinePaper)Available:https://digitalcommons.fiu.edu/cgi/viewcontent.cgi?article=1347&context=sfec. Accessed:11/01/2021

where blacks were always considered as slaves or servants of the white people. This was a difficult situation in which Woods experienced of being forced to take a superior role of the master in his relationship with the black people. Having been brought up among the Xhosa people, Woods identified himself with his Black playmates. Due to immigration most white kids finds it hard to be alienated to their black African friends who are still being discriminated against in the white community. It is time to break the barriers of discrimination and racism which separates us as Apostle Paul declares: Galatians 3:28-29(KJV) ' There is neither Jew nor Greek, there is neither bond nor free, there is neither male nor female: for ye are all one in Christ Jesus. And if ye be Christ's, then are ye Abraham's seed, and heirs according to the promise.'[88]

Still in South Africa Bantu Stephen Biko a South African anti-apartheid activist, an African nationalist and African socialist who also contested against racism and apartheid in South Africa although he went far too extreme in his hatred for injustice. Reid asserts: 'Biko was banned during this entire time but such was the impact of their one-on-one discourse that he was able to grasp for the first time the reality of the apartheid system from the perspective of the victims. In his 1988 presentation
on the subject of apartheid, he shared his fully evolved perspective: I believe nowhere in the world, including the United States, including South Africa or Britain, I don't think White people are capable; and I don't care who they are no matter how sympathetic, how supportive they are to the Black cause. I simply don't think Whites are capable of perceiving completely what it must be like to be in a Black skin in an oppressed society.''[89] It was Biko's

---

[88] Galatians 3:29-29
[89] Merlene V. Reid .(2014) (Perspective Transformation Theory and

opinion that only black people can real understand what black people go through and feel, which may be a strong point of view as white people may not have gone through such discrimination before. Sometimes we learn better through experiencing a situation. Revens, Reynolds, Suclupe, Rifkin and Pierce assert: 'You can never understand a culture until you experience it" [90] This means that sometime we need to experience a situation in order to fully understand it. It is a very common to say that we know what someone else is going through only to try and express our condolence and sympathy to them but the truth is that we really don't understand how they feel as we are all different in processing pain or grief.

It is racial discrimination and inequality that finally facilitated the introduction of ant-semitism and the holocaust in 1934 when Hitler became German's head of state which killed more than 6 million Jewish people. Laws against which worked against the Jewish people were introduced in Germany just as laws against black people were also introduced in US. Steinweis and Rachlin affirm: 'Well-educated , diligent, intelligent, and well-versed in Nazi ideology, Stuckart served as a state Secretary in the Reich Ministry of Interior which exercise important powers over the formulation and implementation of racial laws in the 1930s.'[91] This is an

---

the Donald Woods Experience From Racist to Anti-Apartheid Activist). Prejudice Reduction and Transformation theory (OnlinePaper)Available:https://digitalcommons.fiu.edu/cgi/viewcontent.cgi?article=1347&context=sfec. Accessed:11/01/2021

[90] Keri E. Revens, Andrew D. Reynolds, Roger F. Suclupe, Cameron Rifkin & Taylor Pierce (2018) "You can never understand a culture until you experience it": Journal of Teaching in Social Work,(Online) (Pp 277-291,Available: https://doi.org/10.1080/08841233.2018.1460289 Accessed: 23/01/2021

indication of the craftiness of the law in Germany which was twisted in its interpretation to suppress the Jewish people who lost all their rights as humans.

Racism goes back to the history of Israel where Yahweh the God of Israel identified himself with the nation of Israel: Exodus 3:6 (NIV) 'Then he said, "I am the God of your father, the God of Abraham, the God of Isaac and the God of Jacob."' The nation of Israel had always been the God's chosen nation through Abraham who chose to serve God instead of serving the gods of Mesopotamia./ Er of the Chaldeans. Gordon proclaim: 'Gods other than YAHWEH were worshiped in ancient Israel, and the Old Testament itself is the principal witness of this plurifomity within pre-exilic Israelite religion.'[92] Introducing himself as the God of Abraham, Isaac and Jacob , was the only way in which Yahweh could distinguish himself from many gods which where worshiped in Babylon. This did not mean that God showed discrimination of the people he wanted to fellowship with but at that time only the nation of Israel identified with Him. Guzik proclaims: 'God revealed Himself to Moses by declaring His relationship to the patriarchs. This reminded Moses that God is the God of the covenant, and His covenant with Israel was still valid and important. This wasn't a "new God" meeting Moses, but the same God that dealt with Abraham, Isaac, and Jacob.

i. God would reveal Himself to Moses more intimately than He had to any of the patriarchs; yet it all began with

---

[91] Alan E Steinweis and Robert Rachlin. *The Law in Nazi Germany* .Berghan Books. New York 2013)6

[92] Robert P.Gordon. *The God of Israel*.(Cambridge University Press 2007)3

God reminding Moses of the bridge of covenant they met on.

ii. Some in the days of Moses might have thought that God neglected or forgot His covenant in the 400 years of Israel's slavery in Egypt, since the time of the patriarchs. Nevertheless, God was at work during that time, preserving and multiplying the nation.'[93] This means that God owners the covenant and that he does not forget his promises irrespective of the time or period it might take.

Anti- Semitism goes back to the 9th century in the Pre-Christian anti-Judaism in ancient Greece and Rome . Even in Egypt the Hebrew nation faced racism from the Egyptians where they worked as the slaves of the Egyptians until YAHWEH sent Moses to liberate them from the oppression of the Egyptian Pharaoh. Exodus 3:7 (NIV) 'The LORD said, "I have indeed seen the misery of my people in Egypt. I have heard them crying out because of their slave drivers, and I am concerned about their suffering.'[94][95] Guzik elaborates: 'God wanted Moses and Israel to know His compassionate care for them.'[96] Compassion is one of God's attribute or nature. It doesn't

---

[93] David Guzik(2020),(enduring Word Bible Commentary Philippians)(OnlineBible Commentary) Available: https://enduringword.com/bible-commentary/Exodus-3/ Accessed 12/01/2021

[94] Exodus 3:7

[95] David Guzik(2020),(enduring Word Bible Commentary Philippians)(OnlineBible Commentary) Available: https://enduringword.com/bible-commentary/Exodus-3/ Accessed 12/01/2021

[96] David Guzik(2020),(enduring Word Bible Commentary Philippians)(OnlineBible Commentary) Available: https://enduringword.com/bible-commentary/Exodus-3/ Accessed 12/01/

matter what wrong we may commit against God he remains compassionate if we acknowledge our wrongs and repent.

Racial discrimination and inequality seems to be radicalising the children who are born in this environment as they inherit bitterness and hatred from their parents. Could it be possible that racism is birthing a generation of boys and girls are full of anger who roam the streets of London with knives and guns. This is wrong and should never be justified in any way but it should be conquered with love co-operatively. Racism seem to be having a great impact in the even in the function of human brain. This is manifested when certain individuals begin to hate the colour of their skin .Some people have considered the change of their skin colour so that they can fit in the white community. Myers affirms: 'For centuries the white majority expected the black minority to emulate white standards of beauty or face ridicule. As a result, black people ended up mimicking the values of the white majority, considering light skin better than dark skin and fine, flowing hair better than hair thickly curled.'[97] This looks like (brain washing), or a way of misleading one's mind through deception. Although Michael Jackson had a skin condition which might have contributed to the change of the colour of his skin but it is possible that he also wanted a way of fitting in the white community and as a way of promoting music industry. Racism affects most people in a way that they lose confidence in the colour of their skin. This leads to a mentality that everything that originates from the western world is much better and much godlier that what comes from Africa. Some Africans

---

[97] Jim Myers,. *Afraid of the Dark : What Whites and Blacks Need to Know about Each Other.* Chicago: Lawrence Hill Books. 2000)107

condemned their own African pattern of approaching God and they adopted the western way with the mentality that it is much godlier. Myers goes on asserting: 'Whites are still pleased to hear that black people make these distinctions— and this is more white folly. Black colour prejudices do not mean white standards are universal; rather they reflect how whites have been an oppressive majority and forced blacks to accept views that serve white self-interest.' This means that it pleases those with an oppressive mentality to see the oppressed people remain under oppression so that they can remain dependent on them. This is related to the situation in which people did not expect that the Messiah could come from Nazareth a city that was much despised at that time. John 1:46 (KJV) 'And Nathanael said unto him, can there any good thing come out of Nazareth? Philip saith unto him, Come and see.'"[98] Nazareth was the most marginalised valley in a despised province of a conquered land and nothing good was expected to come out of Nazareth just as the African continent may be despised at this day and age.

Despising the look of our skin appears to be an insult to the creator. This is a call to begin to like what we are created to be. Myers declares: 'The 1960s produced a counterbalancing consciousness movement with its message "Black is beautiful" and brought about an awakening on both sides of the colour line. Across black America, programs were undertaken to encourage black youngsters to have pride in their history and cultural heritage.'[99] This indicates that the black people began to be confident in the colour of their skin. Mostly it is not the white people who are to be blamed for how black people

---

[98] John 1:46
[99] Myers, Jim.. *Afraid of the Dark : What Whites and Blacks Need to Know about Each Other*. Chicago: Lawrence Hill Books.200)113

feel but the black people for not being proud and confident on the colour of their skin. What matters is not what they said or think about you but what matters is what you say and think about yourself. Colonisation is sometimes in our mentality and not in the physical. All we need is to liberate ourselves and stop blaming other people for the damage we bring to ourselves by the way we think and talk about ourselves. At times racism is only in our state of mind and not what they say or do to us.

We have in input in liberating ourselves from the mentality of racism. No matter how others may try to talk us out of low self-esteem, racism mentality and self-pity but what matters is our own self-motivation. Helmstetter declares: 'All external motivation is temporal. External motivation is the kind that may work you up, but it will not keep you awake for long. External motivation is motivation that comes to you from the outside. It may influence you to make a change, but it cannot make a change for you. And it cannot keep you from drifting off course when the motivator is gone.' In the subject of self - esteem this means that it matters to motivate ourselves than depending on other people to talk us out of poor self - esteem of racism and self -discrimination. Even Job declared in Job 22:28(K J V) 'Thou shalt also decree a thing, and it shall be established unto thee: (You shall decree a thing and it shall be established.' This means that our words do have a creative power. We can actually recreate a new environment for ourselves by the words of our own mouth.

Lorne declares: 'This overarching concern with discrimination and diversity has certainly been part of the broader public conversations around race and racism have become increasingly sophisticated over the years. However, when religion and religious discrimination are addressed, they are addressed superficially or they are conflated uncritically with race and racism.'[100] This is reflects the desire to distinguish the politically and racial influenced religious phenomena. For any reason there is no justification for brutality and terrorism in the world and it should be identified and punished accordingly in order to eradicate it which is the aim of this book to investigate the possible causes of violence inequality and discrimination in our nations. Anderson asserts: 'Ethnographic researchers, however, have been trained to look for and to recognize underlying assumptions, their own their own and those of their subjects, and to try to override the former and uncover the latter.'[101] This shows how we aim to uncover the underlying assumptions that cause evil in our communities.

Jackson asserts: 'Racism, like terrorism, is a learned idea, not a born trait. A person will potentially be a racist if she/he comes from a racist environment.'[102] This is a call to take up the responsibility of recreating a new environment without racism in which to bring up the new generation of people. If racism can be learned, then it can be unlearned. Henze, Katz, Norte, Sather and Walker declare: ' A relatively new lens for understanding the roots of interethnic and racial conflict that offers a very pragmatic, yet ultimately hopeful approach, is that of unlearning racism.'[103] This explains the possibility of unlearning racism which might have been passed on from the past generations. Co-operatively it is possible to hand

---

[100] Paul Bramadat and Lorne Dawson ,*Religious radicalization in Canada and beyond*, (University Of Toronto Press 2014)8

[101] Elijah Anderson *Code of the Street Decency, Violence and the Moral life of the Inner city* (W.W. Norton and Company Ltd .London 2000)11

[102] Glenn Erwin Jackson *Surviving the radicalization of America* (iUniverse Lincoln 2005)11

[103] Rosemary Henze, Anne Katz Edmundo Norte, Susan E Sather and Ernest Walker. *Leading For Diversity* 22.

over a beautiful new world of a nonviolent, equality and diversity to the next generations. Henze, Katz , Norte, Sather and Walker draws from the confession of McIntosh who asserted that: 'As a white person, I realized I had been taught racism as something which puts others at a disadvantage, but had been taught not to see its corollary aspect, white privilege, which puts me at an advantage ... I have come to see white privilege as a package of uncarned assets which I can count on cashing in each day, but about which I was meant to remain obvious.'[104] McIntosh was expressing the unfortunate situation of practising racism in he had learned from those who were before him. This proves the fact that the practice of racism is passed on from each generation to the next. This cannot stop until the other generation put a stop to it and start passing on equality and diversity to the generations to come.

Henze, Katz , Norte, Sather and Walker goes on affirming: 'When we realize that racism and its effects are part of the water we swim in- no matter what ethnicity we claim and what colour of our skin is – We are in a position to begin the next stage of our internal journey, unlearning racism.'[105] This is an indication that everyone remains with the responsibility to stop racism as it affect us all in one way or another. Henze, Katz, Norte, Santher and walker draws from Robins and Terrell who asserted that: ' this process may not be easy or comfortable, yet it is ultimately necessary to go through the process of unlearning racism and arrive at what they term "cultural

---

[104] Rosemary Henze, Anne Katz Edmundo Norte, Susan E Sather and Ernest Walker. *Leading For Diversity* 21-22
[105] Rosemary Henze, Anne Katz Edmundo Norte, Susan E Sather and Ernest Walker. Leading For Diversity (Sage Publications Company. London 2002)22

proficiency". This shows us that unlearning racism will take sacrifice and determination as it will not come easy. This will involve humility in working with multicultural collaboration groups and recruiting diverse staff in our schools to promote equality and diversity.

Kivel declares: 'I think it is crucial that each of us speaks up about issues of violence and injustice. It is true that our words will have more moral credibility if we were leading a mistake-free life and were totally consistent in what we say and do. We have to "walk the walk" and not just "talk the talk".[106] This encourages us to practice what we preach about racism if we are to uproot racism totally.

It is clear that in this generation both white and black, Asian or other have all suffered in one way or other consequences of racism which were passed on by those who were before us. We have lost our beloved ones through terrorism which appears to be the result of racial or religious hatred. Kivel asserts: 'The disadvantages of being a person of colour in the United States today include personal insults, harassment, discrimination, economic and cultural exploitation, stereotypes and invisibility, as well as threats, intimidation and violence.'[107] This makes it clear how most black people are harassed, insulted and discriminated, exploited intimidated on a daily basis because of the colour of their skin. Kevel goes on asserting: 'Many of them have been discouraged or prevented from pursuing academic or work goals or have been placed in lower vocational levels because of their racial identity.'[108] This is very true as many black people

---

[106] Paul Kivel, *Uprooting racism* . (New society Publishers .Canada 2011)4

[107] Paul Kivel, *Uprooting racism* . (New society Publishers .Canada 2011)44

[108] Paul Kivel, *Uprooting racism* . (New society Publishers .Canada

encounter discouragements from those who should be encouraging them.

We live in a world that does not guarantee us a sense of belonging, a world of injustice, inequality, racism and favouritism. A world in which if the minority get involved in a dispute with a white person and the police get involved, It is the one from the ethnic minority who is found guilty and taken into police custody. A world in which when there is a domestic dispute, it is the man who is Isolated from his family or given a prison sentence. By this I am not condoning domestic abuse and violence at all as it is wrong and against humanity morals. Glants draws from the works of Krivdina and Antokolsky who commented on the situation of the Jews who lived in Russia: 'It was this encouragement from the government combined with exhortation of the Jewish press that produced a new generation of Jews who regarded themselves no longer merely as subjects of the Russian government but as part and parcel of the Russian culture and the Russian people.' This was an unfortunate situation in which the Jewish people found themselves as they even lost their self-esteem and considered themselves as a property of Russian. They even lost a sense of belonging in Russia because of inequality and discrimination they experience.

I personally faced the discouraging comments from one of my University tutors who appeared to instil it in my mind that I wasn't not academic brilliant to pursue the type of course I was studying as white students. Iliyemi tells reflect on Myles Munroe: 'There was another man who became outstanding in our present day in the person of Dr Myles Munroe, who was born in Bahamas. As a small black boy at the age of thirteen, he was despised and verbally abused by his teacher Mr Robinson from Scotland called him black monkey and all kinds of ridiculous in the presence of the whole class. He also said that Myles could not amount to anything of significance in life. But thanks to God and his mother, who encouraged her son that he could do all things through Christ that strengthens a man. This boy summoned courage and took up the challenge as he rose to become the best overall student, not in his class alone but also in the whole school, upon graduation. Later in the future, Dr Myles's books did not only inspire and bless Mr Robinson but brought him to Christ and saved his life-the writings of the same boy he had once written off.'[109] This explains how some black people suffer verbal abuse from their own teachers who could be encouraging the discouraged students instead. It is a wrong mentality to think that a particular race may be academic brilliant than the other. What matters is the environment we create for the two. It is most common that certain people are enrolled in better schools than others of which the two will not produce the same results. Academic brilliance has nothing to do with the colour of skin. Mia draws from former slaves Jones and Allen who challenged racism: "'those who stigmatize us as men, whose baseness is incurable [to] try the experiment of taking a few black children, and cultivate their minds with the same care, and let them have the same prospect in view, as you would wish for your own children, you would find upon the trial, they were not inferior in mental endowments.'"[110] This confirms the fact that intelligence

---

[109] Freeman O. Ileyemi *The power of Purpose* (Page Publishing Inc. New York 2016)11

[110] Bay, and Bay, Mia. *The White Image in the Black Mind : African-American Ideas about White People, 1830-1925.* New York: Oxford University Press 2000)17

has nothing to do with race and that every child have the potential to excel and do better if they are given equal opportunity.

    Mia continues to challenge the perspective on the African inferiority to the Europeans: 'Turn-of-the-century emancipation day orators also "proclaimed the glories of ancient Egyptian and Ethiopian civilizations." Such claims likewise aimed to counter white racism, while simultaneously reflecting the importance that Africa held in the collective identity of urban free blacks. Such claims likewise aimed to counter white racism, while simultaneously reflecting the importance that Africa held in the collective identity of urban free blacks. Emancipation day orators celebrated their race's African past to disprove the charge, as William Hamilton put it in 1809 , "that we have not produced any poets, mathematicians, or any to excel in any science whatever."'[111] This argues the idea that Africans were inferior civilization originated from free Africans in Egypt and Ethiopia from which the building of pyramids and the irrigation system reveal intelligence which involved geometry, one of the oldest branches of mathematics which was concerned with properties of space that were related with shape, distance, size, and position of figures. Mia proceed: 'In ancient times "our now despised race were the inventors of different arts and sciences, while the rest of the now civilized world were sunk in darkness and ignorance."'[112] It may be pride and arrogance to dispute and try to water down the fact that civilization stated in Africa. It is true that some people have an attitude of

---

[111]Bay, and Bay, Mia. *The White Image in the Black Mind : African-American Ideas about White People, 1830-1925.* 2000)21

[112] Bay, and Bay, Mia. *The White Image in the Black Mind : African-American Ideas about White People, 1830-1925.* 2000)26

superiority is manifested in their overbearing mannerism and assumptions.

Iliyemi again tells a story about Edson: 'At a very tender age, Thomas Edson was sent back home from the school with a note written by his teacher who had already concluded this gut was too stupid to think let alone to learn. Just after three months of formal education, he was totally written off as a young guy without hope and future. This same guy rose up in life to become one of the world's foremost inventors and became high rising in life, not only above his contemporary but also above those that had written him off.'[113] This teaches us never to judge the book by its cover, which means that we should not judge people because of their race, religion or any other outward appearance.

Not only do the black people suffer from the consequences of racism, even white people do suffer from this. From his own experience as a white person, Kivel asserts: 'We also loose the presence and contributions of the people of colour to our neighbourhoods, schools and relationships. Our experiences are distorted, limited and less rich the more they are exclusively or predominantly white.'[114] This shows how the white only community is missing out on the beauty of diversity, richness and talents from other cultures. Racism also deprives white all people including the whites of good relationship with the black people because of tensions caused by racism.

---

[113]Freeman O. Ileyemi The power of Purpose (Page Publishing Inc. New York 2016)11
[114]Paul Kivel, *Uprooting racism* . (New society Publishers .Canada 2011)55

Kivel goes own asserting: 'Racism distorts our sense of danger and safety. We are taught to live in fear of people of color.'[115] This indicates the way racism misguide white people 's emotions to live in fear of people who may be very friendly and caring. Many black people into health care jobs which may reveal that they are loving, caring and friendly in their nature.

Again Kevel asserts: 'We are exploited economically by the ruling class and unable to fight or even to see this exploitation because we are taught to scapegoat people of color.'[116] This suggest that the ruling class may be using the 'divide and rule tactic' by which they maintain control over the poor by encouraging racism between them and the black people as a way of preventing them from uniting in opposition. Instead their attention is diverted to fighting and hatred against the harmless and innocent black people. Not only is that, but feelings of shame, guilt, and embarrassment for being interpreted as people of racism lower self-esteem as racism makes a mockery of the white people's reputation of democracy, equality and justice. Due to wars and persecution, most African people sought for refuge from countries in the west because of their good reputation of promoting life and respecting human rights. Instead when they face racism from people they expected protection it causes the black people to lose respect of the white people.

Yanco further declares: 'It is important to realize that racism is deeply implicated in the scourges of militarism

---

[115] Paul Kivel, *Uprooting racism* . (New society Publishers .Canada 2011)56

[116] Paul Kivel, *Uprooting racism* . (New society Publishers .Canada 2011)56

and materialism. It undergirds the belief that some are more deserving than others, that it is okay to visit violence on certain "others," be that the violence of drone attacks or the withholding of a fair share of the earth's resources.'[117] This indicates that it is not a good thing to use autocratic powers like military and manipulation to oppress and discriminate other people. All humans need to be treated equally with fairness regardless of their race.

Immigration and diversity

Due to immigration today's world has become so diverse in its population culture, religions and many other. Diversity commit to recognizing the variety of characteristics that make individuals unique. Having the mentality of diversity creates an atmosphere that celebrates and promotes individual and collective achievements. Diversity is open to variety of perspectives which are helpful in the development of our nations and the entire world. Today's world has become open minded promoting diversity in our societies. Elaborating on the subject of diversity Titley and Lentin asserts: 'Such language is now common within European union institutions as well as in many of its member states. Interestingly "diversity talk" is also in the rise in France, a country traditionally opposed to the recognition of ethnic minorities and which remains attached to the idea that the nom of equality prohibits the taking into account the religious, ethnic or other differences in circumstances.'[118] This elaborates the way European countries have

---

[117]Yanco, Jennifer J... *Misremembering Dr. King : Revisiting the Legacy of Martin Luther King Jr.*)51

[118]Gavan Titley and Alana Lentin(eds) ,*The Politics of Diversity in Europe.*(Council of Europe Publishing 2008) 31

undergone great transformation to embrace equality and diversity.

Legislation, Equality and Diversity.

It is amazing that with passing of time nations have come to understand and to agree on the legislation that promotes equality and diversity. Hoffman asserts: 'The European convention has to be set principally in the historical context of the aftermath of the second world war(1939-45) and the atrocities committed by, in particular, Nazi Germany, which brutally tortured and murdered millions of people , including several millions of its own citizens, such as Jews, Gypsies, blacks, homosexuals, the disabled, and political dissidents.'[119] Hoffman explains that it was for the reason of safeguarding humans from such cruelty, torture, inhuman or degrading punishment that the Human rights were adopted by the European convention. This became a basis for the Human Rights Act 1998 which safeguard basic rights like a right to life, a right to freedom from torture or inhuman degradation or punishment, a right to freedom from slavery, or forced labour, a right to liberty, a right to a fair trial, a right to access education and many other rights which promotes equality and diversity.

Millam goes on elaborating: 'The Human Rights Act 1998 is based on the European Convention on Human Rights. This is a European charter that deals with civil and political rights. Because of this charter, people in Britain have been able to take human rights issues to the European courts. Now that the Human Rights Act has

---

[119]David Hoffman, John Jermyn Rowe · *Human Rights in the UK, An introduction to the Human Rights Act 1998* (Pearson Education Limited .Essex 2006) 24

been incorporated into the legal systems of United Kingdom, Individuals no longer no longer need to take their cases to the European court of Human Rights in Strasbourg; they can now be heard in Britain courts.'[120] It is certainly a good thing that the human rights were incorporated into the legal system of United Kingdom especially at this time that Britain is out and no longer bound by the laws of the European Union. It still remains illegal to breach the Human Rights.

According to Nolan the Race Relations Act 1976 makes it unlawful to discriminate on 'racial grounds' in employment, housing or services. This includes colour, race, nationality, ethnic or national origins. The Act makes it an offence to incite or encourage racial hatred. This highlights the fact that it is unlawful to discriminate other people on housing or other services on racial grounds.

It is in the consideration of equality and diversity that even employers considers equal pay for their employees. Nolan elaborates on the Equal Pay Act 1970: 'This Act made it unlawful for employers to discriminate between men and women in terms of their pay and conditions of work. Before this law was passed it was possible for an employer to pay men more that women –even though they were doing the same job.'[121] This makes it a crime to discriminate workers because of their gender, race, class, religion, sexuality, politics and many other issues. This enforces equal treatment of all people at work.

---

[120] Rosalind Millam. Anti-discriminatory Practice (Continuum London 2002)24
[121] Yvonne Nolan S/NVQ Level 3 .*Health And Social Care* British Library Heinemann.Debby 2006) 176

Stereotyping assumes that certain group of people are the same. Because of a few black people who were found to be under the influence of illegal drugs it is mostly assumed that all black people deal with illegal drugs and crime. Morey, and Yaqin, asserts: '"Cultural diversity." "Multiethnicity." "Multiculturalism." Call it what you will, nations and their politicians have been debating its viability or failure ever since 9/11. The crucial question being asked is whether cultural difference can be harmonized and a multicultural society created or sustained, or whether the experiment of respecting and attempting politically to include identity positions with values that may jar with those of the majority is a doomed enterprise.'[122] The possibility of a multiracial society comes to a stake because of terrorism. This mentality assumes that certain nationalities of people are most likely to be associated with violence and terrorism. This way of thinking facilitates racial discrimination and inequality within our communities. Morey, and Yaqin further declare: 'Too often while saying Islam is "medieval" its critics overlook the fact that they themselves are indulging in stereotyping that has its roots in the Middle Ages.'[123] This suggests that we should not make haste generalisation over one insufficient piece of evidence from the past, instead we should consider all of the variables. Masey asserts: 'We tend to stereotype those who are most different from ourselves because we understand them less well- a rule that holds true for type differences as well as cultural, racial, etc.'[124] This reflects

---

[122] Peter Morey and Amina Yaqin. *Framing Muslims : Stereotyping and Representation after 9/11.* Cambridge: Harvard University Press.2011)44

[123] Peter Morey and Amina Yaqin. *Framing Muslims : Stereotyping and Representation after 9/11.* Cambridge: Harvard University Press.2011)13

a way of judging people by their appearance instead of seeking to find out more about them.

Still on the anti-discriminatory procedures we refer to United Nations Convention on the Rights of the Child (1989) According to Milliam this has no legal standing although it is known to be an ethical code world wide. Among its 54 articles many of them covers ant-discriminatory practice. Millan asserts: Article 2 says: State Parties shall respect and ensure the rights set forth in the present Convention to each Child within their jurisdiction without discrimination of any kind, irrespective of the child's or his or her parent's or legal guardian's race, colour, sex , language, religion, political or other opinion, national, ethnic or social origin, property, disability, birth or other status'[125] This is a great way of creating a new environment of an anti-discriminatory communities for the coming generations.

Disability Discrimination Act 1995, the Human Rights Act 1998, the Schools Standards and Framework Act 1998 and the Care Standards Act 2000,

Millam asserts: 'Subsequent legislation, including the Disability Discrimination Act 1995 , the Human Rights Act 1998, the Schools Standards and Framework Act 1998 and the Care Standards Act 2000, all require workers to work within an anti-discriminatory framework with

---

[124] Brent Massey.*Where In the World Do I belong.*(UK Jetlag press 2006)11
[125] Rosalind Millam. *Anti-discriminatory Practice* (Continuum London 2002)28

children, young people, families, adults, colleagues and other professionals.'[126] This indicates that it has become a legal obligation for everyone to work in the anti-discriminatory framework. Being a legal obligation to work within the framework of anti-discrimination does not guarantee an environment free of discrimination as we continue to experience this phenomenon and challenge in our everyday lives. It is high time we acknowledge and address individuals and various groups' needs in our societies. There is a need to consider factors like gender, age, sexual orientation, disability, race, religion, culture and many more. Millam goes on asserting: 'Anti-discriminatory practice actively takes account of the many different facets of individuals and groups and acknowledges them in all aspects of work.'[127] This may mean that people may be treated differently according to their individual circumstances.

The Equality Act 2010 and UN Convention

This Act protects people from being discriminated against in terms of employment, education, access to goods, services and facilities and even in buying and renting land or property.

This Act promotes and protect the rights of disabled people at the same time protecting people's rights if they have an association with a disabled person, for example a parent or a carer. From online: 'Equality Act provisions which came into force on 1 October 2010:

---

[126] Rosalind Millam. *Anti-discriminatory Practice* (Continuum London 2002) viii

[127] Rosalind Millam. *Anti-discriminatory Practice* (Continuum London 2002) x-ix

The basic framework of protection against direct and indirect discrimination, harassment and victimisation in services and public functions, premi, work, education, associations and transport

changing the definition of gender reassignment, by removing the requirement for medical supervision

providing protection for people discriminated against because they are perceived to have, or are associated with someone who has, a protected characteristic

clearer protection for breastfeeding mothers

applying a uniform definition of indirect discrimination to all protected characteristics

harmonising provisions allowing voluntary positive action

Provisions relating to disability

extending protection against indirect discrimination to disability

introducing the concept of "discrimination arising from disability" to replace protection under previous legislation lost as a result of a legal judgment

applying the detriment model to victimisation protection (aligning with the approach in employment law)

harmonising the thresholds for the duty to make reasonable adjustments for disabled people

extending protection against harassment of employees by third parties to all protected characteristics

making it more difficult for disabled people to be unfairly screened out when applying for jobs, by restricting the circumstances in which employers can ask job applicants questions about disability or health

Provisions relating to work'[128] This means that it is against the law to discriminate people in their way of life.

---

[128] Guidance Equality Act 2010: 27 February 2013. Government Equalities Office and Equality and Human Rights Commission.

Millam goes on examining the Education Reform Act 1998: 'The Education Reform Act brought about major changes to the education system, with one of the most significant being the introduction of the National Curriculum. This stipulates that schools must offer a curriculum that is balanced and broadly based and that it should: (A) promote the spiritual, moral, cultural, mental and physical development of pupils at school and in society; and (b) prepare such pupils for the opportunities, responsibilities and experiences of adult life.'[129] This reveals the effort by the education system to try and eliminate inequality and racial discrimination by balancing its education system.

In actual sense it is possible that black people or white people may not actual come to the understanding of each other until they give themselves to relate with each other deeply. What we see or think about each other may not be their true identity. Mia affirms: 'Europeans encountering Africans within the context of the international slave trade saw black people as brutish and bestial. As historian Winthrop Jordan observes, the parallels Europeans drew between Africans and apes may have received their initial impulse from the coincidence that some Europeans first encountered both black people and some of the most human-looking animals of the simian species at the same time and in the same part of the world.'[130] This explains that some Europeans justified

---

Available: https://www.gov.uk/guidance/equality-act-2010-guidance. Accessed: 27/09/2021

[129] Rosalind Millam. *Anti-discriminatory Practice* (Continuum London 2002)19

taken Africans for slavery because they considered them to be animals rather than human beings. It is a shame that these European did not first consider doing a research or relating with black people in order to understand them. However this way of reasoning was challenged as Mia goes on asserting: 'The men and women in the antislavery movement reaffirmed the traditional scriptural conception of all people as children of God. And they posed environmental explanations of the Negro's color and physiognomy to those who sought to argue that Africans were both so degraded and so different from Europeans that they should be seen as a lower species of people, suited only for perpetual slavery.'[131] This explains that all people regardless of the colour of their skin, they were all created in the image of God and no one should be seen as being inferior to the other.

Mia challenges racism as they draw from Forten: 'From the late eighteenth century onward, blacks protesting slavery and racial discrimination pointedly reaffirmed the legitimate place of their race in the human species and cited the physical and mental characteristics shared by both races as evidence. "Has the god who made the white man and the black, left any record declaring us a different species?" asked black Philadelphian James Forten in 1813 . "Are we not sustained by the same power, supported by the same food, hurt by the same wounds, wounded by the same wrongs, pleased by the same delights, and propagated by the same means?"'[132] This

---

[130] Bay, and Bay, Mia. *The White Image in the Black Mind : African-American Ideas about White People, 1830-1925.* New York: Oxford University Press,2000)4

[131] Bay, and Bay, Mia. *The White Image in the Black Mind : African-American Ideas about White People, 1830-1925.* 2000)19

[132] Bay, and Bay, Mia. *The White Image in the Black Mind : African-*

affirms that all humans share the same physical and mental characteristics and therefore there shouldn't be any reason for racial discrimination and inequality at all. Mia draws from Ennels and Bell : 'A difference in color is not a difference of species. Our structure and organization are the same, and not distinct from other men; in what respects are we inferior?'" This was a strong argument by Ennels and Bell that Africans may be inferior to white people.

This is also true of the Africans who considered white people as carnivores just because they appeared strange to them. Mia further assert: 'Similarly, African fears about white cannibalism were rooted in a very specific historical context. As William Piersen points out, these fears had "antecedents in traditional African tribal animosities that placed the imputation of cannibalism on distrusted foreign peoples." Moreover, African fears about cannibalism also arose from the circumstance that Africans taken by the Europeans were usually never seen again. One captured African reported that his people, the Foleys of West Africa, had a great horror "for the state of slavery amongst the English; for they generally imagined, that all who were sold for slaves, were generally eaten or murdered, since none had ever returned."'[133] The slaves who were taken from Africa were never returned back to Africa as some died along the way as living conditions in which they were transported were not conducive at all. Just because the slaves never returned back to Africa, Africans actually thought that they were being eaten as meat on arrival. Labelling attaches a descriptive word

---

American Ideas about White People, 1830-1925. 2000)20
[133] *Bay, and Bay, Mia. The White Image in the Black Mind : African-American Ideas about White People, 1830-1925. 2000)4*

certain people. This happens because of not having enough knowledge about that individual.

It is important to avoid prejudices in our daily interactions with other people of different race. At times our own feeling about the other person can mislead us as prejudice may cause a feeling towards other people based on their apparent group. This is a result of our own values and beliefs which may conflict our relationship with others. We all have the potential to liberate ourselves from being victims of prejudice by standing up for ourselves and proving the racial abusers wrong. Mia declares: 'as daughters of a despised race, to use our utmost endeavours to enlighten the understanding, to cultivate the talents entrusted to our keeping, that by so doing, we may in a great measure, break down the strong barrier of prejudice, and raise ourselves to an equality with those of our fellow beings, who differ from us in complexion.'"[134] This means that even woman from the minority ethnic group should stand up for themselves and discover the potential and talents which God allocated to each one of us. It is our responsibility to remove the stigma that is put on us because of our looks as Mia declares further: "'unmerited stigma attempted to be cast upon the reputation of the free people of color.'"[135] This indicates that there is a negative mentality and opinion about the black people which is not their true identity.

This leads us to the term Labelling, This is more like stereotyping but this is slightly complex as this attaches a

---

[134] Bay, and Bay, Mia. *The White Image in the Black Mind : African-American Ideas about White People, 1830-1925.* New York: Oxford University Press,2000)22

[135] Bay, and Bay, Mia. *The White Image in the Black Mind : African-American Ideas about White People, 1830-1925.* 2000)24

descriptive word or phrase to certain people or things based on a certain experience. For example when a black person is arrested, some people label them as criminals even before they are found guilty or charged. Labelling categorises and passes judgements on certain people based on the past. This creates stereotypes, stigma, hearsay, fears bias, and the inability to separate that individual from the label we put on them resulting to racial discrimination and inequality. Nolan goes on asserting: 'Labelling happens when someone thinks the factor which people have in common is more important than the hundreds of factors which make them different.'[136] This is when we focus on what is wrong to define or judge individuals. Labelling leads to discrimination and abuse. We begin to call people names which seem to define or describe their challenges. I lived among a certain tribe that did not speak my language . Each time I tried to pronounce certain words, other students laughed at me and called me that particular pronunciation. This destroyed my self-esteem and I did not want to try learning that particular language for quite a long time.

We cannot discuss the subject of diversity without examining discrimination which has proved to be a great hindrance to equality and diversity. Nolan elaborates: discrimination means treating some categories of people less well than others. People are often discriminated against because of their race, beliefs, gender, religion, sexuality or age.'[137] It is true that treating people as of a lesser value than others is a form of discrimination but I wonder if treating all people in the same way is not a form of discrimination as well. For example it is not a good thing to treat the disable people in the same way we treat

---

[136] Yvonne Nolan 2006)196
[137] Yvonne Nolan 2006)196

everyone. At times we might need to consider the wheel chair access into our public buildings or offices. Thompson proclaims: 'Discrimination is therefore a sociological and political phenomenon as well as a psychological one ..'[138] This indicates a need for a change in the pattern of thinking as discrimination is birthed in a way of our reasoning. Solomon declares: Proverbs 23:7 (King James Version) ' For as he thinketh in his heart, so is he.'[139] This indicates the fact that we are the products of what we constantly think about.

Thompson declares: 'Where there is difference, there is the potential for unfair discrimination, in so far as it creates the potential for particular individuals or groups to be identified as 'different' and therefore treated less favourably.'[140] This explains that people are different and characterised by diversity and therefore likely to be treated differently Nolan goes on explains the Disability Discrimination Act 1995: 'This Act is designed to prevent discrimination against people with disabilities in employment, access to education and transport, housing and obtaining goods and services. Employers and landlords must not treat a disabled person less favourably than a non-disabled person.'[141] This means that it is against the law to discriminate people because of their condition or disability.

This leads us to Anti-discrimination topic in which we explore the ways and ideas of eliminating and challenging

---

[138] Neil Thompson. *Anti-Discriminatory Practice: Equality, Diversity and Social Justice* Palgrave .UK 2016)8
[139] Prov 23:7
[140]Neil Thompson. *Anti-Discriminatory Practice: Equality, Diversity and Social Justice* Palgrave .UK 2016)5
[141]Yvonne Nolan 2006)177

discrimination in our nations. As I mentioned before that in our buildings we need to consider the wheelchair users and many other. In our multi-cultural Churches, or government/ council offices we need to consider involving interpreters to make sure that no one feels left out because of the language they speak. Thompson asserts: 'Despite the progress made in developing our awareness of discrimination and oppression and developing anti-discriminatory approaches to theory, practice and education, there is no room for complacency.'[142] This is an encouragement to keep on thriving in working against discrimination and oppression.

Thompson further asserts: 'Anti-discriminatory practice is a matter of a principled commitment to equality, diversity and social justice, rather than simply following political, intellectual, or other fashions.'[143] This means that we must not only enjoy talking about anti-discrimination without practically implementing what we teach or talk about.

Thompson goes on proclaiming: 'We therefore need to develop quite a sophisticated level of understanding of the complexities involved, rather than look for simple solutions that can be both woefully inadequate (in terms of not doing justice to the intricacies of what we are dealing with) and potentially disastrous (in terms of making the situation worse).'[144] This means making a sacrifice to do what it takes to deal with discrimination and inequality although it may not be an easy way.

---

[142] Neil Thompson *Anti-Discriminatory Practice: Equality, Diversity and Social Justice* Palgrave .UK 2016)2

[143] Neil Thompson. *Anti-Discriminatory Practice: Equality, Diversity and Social Justice* Palgrave .UK 2016)2

[144] Neil Thompson. Anti-Discriminatory Practice: Equality, Diversity and Social Justice Palgrave .UK 2016)7

In his further elaboration Thompson declares: 'when it comes to discrimination and oppression, there is no neutral middle ground. If we are not challenging the unfair ways people are treated, then at best we are implicitly condoning them and may actually be reinforcing them.'[145] This is a challenge to everyone to embrace the responsibility of challenging discrimination in any cost.

Nelson Mandela and the antidiscrimination policy

Mandela' aimed to eliminate apartheid and racism from South Africa. Durrheim asserts: 'It was the ANC's 'ideological lodestar' (Lodge 1983). Examine the select quotes from the Freedom Charter in the box on page 12 which capture the main aim of the struggle, namely, to produce a non-racist society. This required acknowledging that 'our people' have been robbed of their land and liberty, recognising the need to restore these human rights to those who had been dispossessed, and creating a democratic state in which black and white would live together as 'equals, countrymen and brothers'[146]. It is amazing that even after 27 years in prison Mandela remained with the same mentality of living peacefully with foreign nationalities in South Africa. The United Nations article draws from the words of Mandela: 'During my lifetime I have dedicated myself to this struggle of the African people. I have fought against white domination, and I have fought against black domination. I have cherished the ideal of a democratic and free society in

---

[145] Neil Thompson. *Anti-Discriminatory Practice: Equality, Diversity and Social Justice* Palgrave .UK 2016)10

[146] Kevin Durrheim *Race Trouble : Race, Identity and Inequality in Post-Apartheid South Africa*. Lanham, MD: Lexington Books. 2011)17

which all persons live together in harmony and with equal opportunities. It is an ideal which I hope to live for and to achieve. But if needs be, it is an ideal for which I am prepared to die.'[147] This indicates that Mandela was dedicated to promoting peace, dignity and equality in South Africa. One could have expected Mandela to develop anger and demand vengeance against white people as did Mugabe after the Independence of Zimbabwe in 1980. It is because of his attitude that Mandela was well respected world -wide as a man of integrity that even UK named streets after him in honour of his good reputation and legacy.

Elaborating on the ant-discriminatory procedures Durrheim draws from the Freedom Charter: 'We, the People of South Africa, declare for all our country and the world to know: that South Africa belongs to all who live in it, black and white, and that no government can justly claim authority unless it is based on the will of all the people; that our people have been robbed of their birthright to land, liberty and peace by a form of government founded on injustice and inequality; that our country will never be prosperous or free until all our people live in brotherhood, enjoying equal rights and opportunities; that only a democratic state, based on the will of all the people, can secure to all their birthright without distinction of colour, race, sex or belief; And therefore, we, the people of South Africa, black and white together equals, countrymen and brothers adopt this Freedom Charter; And we pledge ourselves to strive together, sparing neither strength nor courage, until the democratic changes here set out have been won.'[148]In

---

[147] United Nations, (Peace, Dignity,and Equality on a healthy planet) Online Article. Available: https://www.un.org/en/site-index accessed:27/09/2021

order to eliminate racial discrimination it is important that the state ensure that people learn to live together as members of the same family. It was a good declaration that South Africa belongs to everyone that lives in it. It was also good that in their declaration the Freedom Charter promised the restoration of equal rights and opportunities, to secure a birth right to all without discrimination of their faith, sex, race or colour of their skin.

Durrheim draws from Habib and Bentley : 'After winning this election, the ANC government introduced legislative measures to eradicate racism. To achieve the vision articulated in the Freedom Charter, the programme of transformation included political democratisation, economic inclusion and the deracialisation of society'[149] Because of the integrity of his personality Mandela honoured the promises of the Freedom Charter and maintained peace with former ruling party of apartheid but it is a shame that after the death of Mandela his successors failed to honour the Freedom Charter pledge, instead South Africa resorted to racism and xenophobia where foreign nationals were killed with the use of burning car tyres.

Equal opportunity Act

Under the Equality Act 2010. all workers within an organisation should be allowed to access all of the organisations facilities at every stage of engagement, including the pre-employment phase. From online: 'To

---

[148]Kevin Durrheim *Race Trouble : Race, Identity and Inequality in Post-Apartheid South Africa.* 2011)17

[149] Durrheim, Kevin. *Race Trouble : Race, Identity and Inequality in Post-Apartheid South Africa.* Lanham, MD: Lexington Books 2011)19

comply with the terms of the Equality Act, employers must have policies in place and must adhere to certain practices that aim to prevent accident claims, discrimination and foster equal opportunities within the organisation.

All workers and job applicants must be treated equally and be given the same set of opportunities regardless of their age, sex, race, disability, sexual orientation, disability, culture or anything other personal characteristic that might be discriminated against.

As a worker, you have a right to:

Fair practices and behaviour in the workplace
Fair allocations of workloads
Equal access to benefits and conditions
A workplace that is free from unlawful discrimination, harassment or bullying at work
Competitive merit-based selection processes for recruitment and promotion
Fair processes to deal with work-related complaints and grievances
If any of these rights are breached or your employment is terminated and you deem it as unfair dismissal an employment solicitor should be able to offer you their expert opinion.'[150] This makes it clear that every human being should get a fair treatment from their work place or else the employer may be breaking the law by an act of discrimination.

When discrimination is ok

---

[150] EOC-2021 Definition of Equal Opportunities Under The Equality Available online :https://www.eoc.org.uk/ accessed: 27/09/2021

I wonder if there are circumstances when discrimination is ok. Due to Covid 19 pandemic many people are Isolated from other people giving them time to recover from the Corona virus in Isolation rather than spreading the virus. It look like this has become another way of justifying discrimination in order to protect the public. At one time I went out for a walk to the shops and along the way I saw my neighbour who in the past days was diagnosed with Covid 19. I felt bad as I watched people walking away from this gentleman although he had spent his government allocated fourteen days of Isolation. People did not trust if he was at this time from from the virus. It is obvious that he is now facing discrimination because he had been infected with the virus.

As we round up on anti-discrimination, equality and diversity it is important to understand that we are all related and we all have the same origins as Mia draws from Russwurm: 'The Egyptians, Ethiopians, and their black African descendants, Russwurm emphasized, were descendants of Ham by way of his son Cush, whose progeny left a more illustrious record in biblical history than the white branch of the human family — that is, the descendants of Japhet. From these historical and scriptural arguments for black equality, Russwurm finished with a scientific argument. He asserted that mankind was originally neither black nor white but copper-colored, and that the physical differences between the races were caused by the environment. The ancient Egyptians became black in Africa as a result of the effects of that continent's hot climate on bile. Likewise, Europeans could permanently darken with prolonged exposure to the equatorial sun.'[151] This is evidenced by the historical and

---

[151] Bay, and Bay, Mia. *The White Image in the Black Mind : African-American Ideas about White People, 1830-1925*. New York: Oxford

scriptural evidences that all humans are the same except for the environmental effects that the colour of skin may look different.

Conclusion

It is my greatest desire to create an impartial society, with Equal Opportunities for everyone as I aim to raise an Awareness of equality and injustice across the entire world with the aim to aid organisations to achieve their diversity objectives and which will enable the creation of safe and comfortable environment for people of all genders, ages and races.

Therefore I conclude that it is high time that we overcome all barriers of racial discrimination and inequality that divides us. It is time unite in war against poverty, the coved 19 pandemic and terrorism with the understanding that we are much more stronger together than when we are divided. Leviticus 26:7-8 (NKJV)

'You will chase your enemies, and they shall fall by the sword before you. Five of you shall chase a hundred, and a hundred of you shall put ten thousand to flight; your enemies shall fall by the sword before you.' It is clear that Moses was discouraging divisions among the children of

University Press,2000)27,28

Israel as they travelled from Egypt to their land of promise. This applies to our present generation which faces many obstacles that needs our undivided effort for us to defeat them.

Acknowledgements

I am thankful for constant encouragement, support and guidance from Joyce Holloway and all Teaching staffs of The University of West of Scotland (SBC) which helped me in successfully completing my training. Also, I would like to extend my sincere esteems to Rev Ian Beach for his timely support and encouragement. Above all I give all the glory and honour to the lord Jesus Christ the Father and the Holy Spirit for enabling me to write this piece of work.
May God bless you all.
Finally all blessings to the Student Awards Agency Scotland (SAAS) which gave me a second chance.

About the author

Joseph Gilson is the senior pastor of Joy Ministries (Excellencia Global mission) in the UK and abroad. He is a postgraduate of The University of West Of Scotland and of Africa Multination for Christ University. Joseph holds a degree in Theology and Pastoral studies. He also studied health and social care at Brooksby College in Milton Mowbray and from Leicester College. Joseph also had an experience of working as a Chaplain at Belvedere Manor for MHA. He also had an experience of working alongside the HMP Glenochil prison Chaplain in Scotland. Joseph also works as a Practice Development Facilitator.

joe.gils71@gmail.com

Footnotes

Pep Talk , *Master the Art of Public Speaking.* India.2020,35

²The New Strategist Editors, ed. *Racial and Ethnic Diversity : Asians, Blacks, Hispanics, Native Americans and Whites.* (Amityville: New Strategist Press,2013)2

³ Kathryn Borman, M., and Dorn, Sherma (eds. *Education Reform in Florida : Diversity and Equity in Public Policy.* Ithaca: State University of New York Press. 2007)10

⁴ Gloria Likupe PhD, MSc, PGCEA, BSc (Hons), DipN, RN Uduak Archibong PhD, FWACN, FRCN(Black African Nurses' Experiences of Equality, Racism, and Discrimination in the National Health Service)(Psychological issues in Organisational culture) Wiley Online Library (Oneline)Journal.(Volume3, IssueS1)(Pages 227-246) Available:(https://doi.org/10.1002/jpoc.21071) accessed:14/11/20

[5] Graeme Lockwood, Claire Henderson and Graham Thornicroft (March 2012)(Article/equality-act-2010-and-mental-health) <u>The British Journal of Psychiatry</u> (Online)(Volume 200 , Issue 3,(pp. 182 – 183)Available:DOI: https://doi.org/10.1192/bjp.bp.111.097790) accessed: 01/01/2021

[6] Emphasis: Mine

[7] Rosemary Henze, Anne Katz Edmundo Norte, Susan E Sather and Ernest Walker. *Leading For Diversity* (Sage Publications Company. London 2002)21

[8] John Pendleton (The experiences of black and minority ethnic nurses working in the UK) <u>British Journal of Nursing</u> (Jan 2017) (Online) (VOL. 26, NO. 1) Available: https://doi.org/10.12968/bjon.2017.26.1.37 Accessed:14/11/20

[9] Dyer O.(07 September 2020) (Covid-19: Black people and other minorities are hardest hit in US).<u>The journal of rural health</u>.Online:(Volume36, Issue4) (Pp 602-608)Available: https://doi.org/10.1111/jrh.12511 Accessed:02/01/2021

[10] Bridget Byrne, Claire Alexander, Omar Khan, James Nazro and William Shankley *Ethnicity and Race in the UK: State of the Nation* (Bristol University Press, Policy Press 2020)10

[11] Dyer O.(07 September 2020) (Covid-19: Black people and other minorities are hardest hit in US).<u>The journal of rural health</u>.Online:(Volume36, Issue4) (Pp 602-

608)Available: https://doi.org/10.1111/jrh.12511
Accessed:02/01/2021

[12] Hsiao –Hung Pal and Benjamin Zephaniah,Angry White People.(Zed Books Limited .London.2016) Preview

[13]Lakshay Sood Vanita Sood (MD) (03 May 2020) (Being African American and Rural: A Double Jeopardy From COVID-19) The journal of Rural Health Online (Volume37, Issue1) (Pp 217-221) Available: https://doi.org/10.1111/jrh.12459 Accessed: 02/01/2021

[14]Keith Ferdinand(M.D).,Tivona Batieste and Mashl iFleurestil (M.S).(June 2020)(Contemporary and Future Concepts on Hypertension in African Americans: COVID-19 and Beyond. Journal of the National Medical Association. Online (Volume 112, Issue 3,) (Pages 315-323) Available: https://doi.org/10.1016/j.jnma.2020.05.018 Accessed: 02/01/2021

[15]Harry J.Holzera and JessReaser (Nov 200)(Black Applicants, Black Employees, and Urban Labor Market Policy) Journal of Urban Economics Online:(Volume 48, Issue 3,) (Pp 365-387) Available: https://doi.org/10.1006/juec.2000.2171
Accesed:02/01/2021

[16] Elizabeth Stearnsa ,Nandan Jhaa and Stephanie Potochnick (Race, secondary school course of study, and college type)May 2013 Social Science Research.Online (Volume 42, Issue 3) (Pages 789-803) Available: https://doi.org/10.1016/j.ssresearch.2013.01.007
Accessed:02/01/2021

[17] Taylor, Keeanga-Yamahtta. *From #BlackLivesMatter to Black Liberation.* (Chicago: Haymarket Books.2016)4

[18] Maya Goodfellow *Hostile Environment, How immigrants became scapegoats* (Veso Books. London.2019)50

[19] Maya Goodfellow *Hostile Environment, How immigrants became scapegoats.* 50

[20] Maya Goodfellow *Hostile Environment, How immigrants became scapegoats.* 5

[21] Amelia Gentleman. *The Windrush Betrayal.* (Bloomsbury House. London 2019)1-5

[22] Memmi Albert. *Racism.* (Minneapolis: University of Minnesota Press 1999)10

[23] Colin Webster *Understanding Race and Crime.* Buckingham: McGraw-Hill Education. 2007)3

[24] Colin Webster *Understanding Race and Crime.* Buckingham: McGraw-Hill Education. 2007)6

[25] Memmi Albert. *Racism.*29

[26] Memmi Albert. *Racism.*29

[27] Yanco, Jennifer J... *Misremembering Dr. King : Revisiting the Legacy of Martin Luther King Jr.* (Bloomington: Indiana University Press. 2014)51

[28] Kuhl, Stefan. *The Nazi Connection : Eugenics, American Racism, and German National Socialism.* Cary: Oxford University Press,2002)xiv

[29] Wojciech Piontek 2019 Depopulation in the Concept of Sustainable Development Middle Pomeranian scientific Society Of Environment Protection Rocznik Ochrona Środowiska (Online) Paper Volume 21 (Pp 523-542 Available: https://ros.edu.pl/images/roczniki/2019/032_ROS_V21_R2019.pdf Accessed:12/01/2021

[30] Genesis 1:28

[31] Wojciech Piontek 2019 Depopulation in the Concept of Sustainable Development Middle Pomeranian scientific Society Of Environment Protection Rocznik Ochrona Środowiska (Online) Paper Volume 21 (Pp 524 Available: https://ros.edu.pl/images/roczniki/2019/032_ROS_V21_R2019.pdf Accessed:12/01/2021

[32] Wojciech Piontek 2019 Depopulation in the Concept of Sustainable Development Middle Pomeranian scientific Society Of Environment Protection Rocznik Ochrona Środowiska (Online) Paper Volume 21 (Pp 523-542 Available: https://ros.edu.pl/images/roczniki/2019/032_ROS_V21_R2019.pdf Accessed:12/01/2021

[33] Tamar Kintsurashvili , Maiko Ratiani 30 April 2020 Does Bill Gates promise us depopulation and chipping? Healthcare/Biosafety Online article .Available: http://www.mythdetector.ge/en/myth/does-bill-gates-promise-us-depopulation-and-chipping Accessed: 12/01/2021

[34] Tamar Kintsurashvili , Maiko Ratiani 30 April 2020 Does Bill Gates promise us depopulation and chipping? Healthcare/Biosafety Online article .Available:

http://www.mythdetector.ge/en/myth/does-bill-gates-promise-us-depopulation-and-chipping Accessed: 12/01/2021

[35] Rueben C. Warren, D.D.S., Dr.P.H., M.Div., Lachlan Forrow, M.D., David Augustin Hodge, Sr., D.Min., Ph.D., and Robert D. Truog, M.D. 16 Oct 2020 Trustworthiness before Trust — Covid-19 Vaccine Trials and the Black The New England Journal of Medicine (Online) Available: https://www.nejm.org/doi/full/10.1056/NEJMp2030033 Accessed: 12/01/2021

[36] Yanco, Jennifer J... Misremembering Dr. King : Revisiting the Legacy of Martin Luther King)54

[37] Emphasis: Mine

[38] Yanco, Jennifer J... Misremembering Dr. King : Revisiting the Legacy of Martin Luther King)55

[39] Yanco, Jennifer J... Misremembering Dr. King : Revisiting the Legacy of Martin Luther King)55

[40] Alexander Smith, Feb. 10, 2020, Article : (Meghan Markle and British racism)online : available: https://www.nbcnews.com/news/world/meghan-markle-british-racism-what-her-saga-says-black-britons-n1132181 Accessed: 27/09/2021

[41] Alexander Smith, Feb. 10, 2020, Article : (Meghan Markle and British racism)online : available: https://www.nbcnews.com/news/world/meghan-markle-british-racism-what-her-saga-says-black-britons-n1132181 Accessed: 27/09/2021

42 Tom Spiggle, Mar 23, 2021,(What Meghan Markle's Experiences Tell Us About Mental Health And Racism At Work.)Online . Available: https://www.forbes.com/sites/tomspiggle/2021/03/23/what-meghan-markles-experiences-tell-us-about-mental-health-and-racism-at-work/?sh=12f67d083fa3 Accessed: 27/09/2021

43 Mikhaila Friel and Rachel Hosie Insider. Mar 10, 2021, (The British royal family has turned a blind eye to its racist past) Online article. Available: https://www.insider.com/british-royal-family-racist-history-black-lives-matter-2020-8 Accessed: 27/09/2021

44 Taylor and Francis Group. (Politics and Religion in Zimbabwe.) Online article: available: https://www.taylorfrancis.com/chapters/edit/10.4324/9780367823993-12/robert-gabriel-mugabe-black-african-theologian-philosopher-robert-matikiti accessed: 27/09/2021

45 Matondi, Prosper B... *Zimbabwe's Fast Track Land Reform.*(London: Zed Books. 2012)xi

46 Moyo, Sam, and Chambati, Walter, eds. (Land and Agrarian Reform in Zimbabwe : Beyond White-Settler Capitalism. Dakar: Codesria 2013)30

47 Moyo, Sam, Chambati and Walter, eds. *(Land and Agrarian Reform in Zimbabwe*)32 ,33

48 Moyo, Sam, Chambati and Walter, eds. (Land and Agrarian Reform in Zimbabwe)35

49 Gal 3:27-28

[50]Rosario Rodriguez, Ruben.*Racism and God-Talk: A Latino/a Perspective.*(NYU Press, 2008)1

[51]Rosario Rodriguez, Ruben Racism and God-Talk: A Latino/a Perspective.)3,4

[52]Rosario Rodriguez, Ruben *Racism and God-Talk: A Latino/a Perspective.*)3

[53]Rosario Rodriguez, Ruben Racism and God-Talk: A Latino/a Perspective.)4

[54] Milles Tribble and Valerie A. *Change Agent Church in Black Lives Matter Times:Urgency* Fortress Academic 2020)7

[55]Milles Tribble and Valerie A. *Change Agent Church in Black Lives Matter Times:Urgency*,8

[56]Taylor, Keeanga-Yamahtta. *From #BlackLivesMatter to Black Liberation.* (Chicago: Haymarket Books.2016)3

[57] Taylor, Keeanga-Yamahtta. From #BlackLivesMatter to Black Liberation. (Chicago: Haymarket Books.2016)6

[58]Yanco, Jennifer J... Misremembering Dr. King : Revisiting the Legacy of Martin Luther King)54

[59]Ben Riley-Smith, Rozina Sabur and Nick Allen. (8 January 2021) Five dead in US Capitol riot after Donald Trump's supporters storm Washington) USA, (US Election, US Politics, Donald Trump The telegraph, Online, available : https://www.telegraph.co.uk/news/2021/01/08/us-capitol-

riot-protest-what-happened-who-died-trump-supporters/
Accessed :08/01/21

[60]Pete Marovich (06/01/21) (The Presidential Transition)The New York Times Online . Available: https://www.nytimes.com/2021/01/06/us/politics/trump-speech-capitol.html Accessed: 08/01/21

[61] Sean Malloy, L. *Out of Oakland : Black Panther Party Internationalism during the Cold War.* Ithaca: Cornell University Press. 2017)241
[62]Sean Malloy, L. Out of Oakland : Black Panther Party Internationalism during the Cold War. Ithaca: Cornell University Press. 2017)241

[63]Al Gini Ronald M. Green. (25 March 2013) Abraham Lincoln/Rosa Parks: Moral.Wiley online library Available: https://doi-org.dtl.idm.oclc.org/10.1002/9781118551653.ch7 Accessed: 10/01/2021

[64] Jeanne Theoharis, *The Rebellious Life of Mrs. Rosa Parks* (Beacon Press Massachusetts 2013)x

[65]Fredrickson, George M., and Fredrickson, George M..*Big Enough to Be Inconsistent : Abraham Lincoln Confronts Slavery and Race.* Cambridge: Harvard University Press.2008)18

[66] Kenneth Mostern . *Autobiography and Black Identity Politics : Racialization in Twentieth-Century America.* Cambridge: Cambridge University Press.1999)149

[67] Michele Gillespie, and McMillen, Sally G., eds. *North Carolina Women : Their Lives and Times, Volume 2.* Athens: University of Georgia Press.2015)263

[68]Cohen, Warren I. *Profiles in Humanity : The Battle for Peace, Freedom, Equality, and Human Rights.*)27.

[69] Zamalin, Alex. *Struggle on Their Minds : The Political Thought of African American Resistance.* New York: Columbia University Press.2017)120

[70]Kane, John. *The Politics of Moral Capital.* (Cambridge: Cambridge University Press.2001)149

[71]Cohen, Warren I.(*Profiles in Humanity : The Battle for Peace, Freedom, Equality, and Human Rights.* Lanham, MD: Rowman & Littlefield Publishers 2009)91

[72] Morgan Ndlovu (2017) Manufacturing Black-on-Black Violence in Africa: A Decolonial Perspective on Mfecane and Afrophobia/Xenophobia in South Africa, International Journal of African Renaissance Studies - Multi-, Inter- and Transdisciplinarity, 12:2, 97-109, DOI: 10.1080/18186874.2017.1401768. Accessed: 27/09/2021

[73]Cohen, Warren I. *Profiles in Humanity : The Battle for Peace, Freedom, Equality, and Human Rights.* (Lanham, MD: Rowman & Littlefield Publishers.2009)134

[74] Crush, Jonathan, Chikanda, Abel, and Skinner, Caroline, eds. *Mean Streets : Migration, Xenophobia and Informality in South Africa.* Cape Town: (Southern African Migration Programme (SAMP)2015)5.

[75]Yanco, Jennifer J... Misremembering Dr. King : Revisiting the Legacy of Martin Luther King Jr.)52

[78]Crush, Jonathan, Chikanda, Abel, and Skinner, Caroline,(eds). *Mean Streets : Migration, Xenophobia and Informality in South Africa.*)5.

[79] Crush, Jonathan, Chikanda, Abel, and Skinner, Caroline,(eds). Mean Streets : Migration, Xenophobia and Informality in South Africa.)7.

[80] Crush, Jonathan, Chikanda, Abel, and Skinner, Caroline,(eds). Mean Streets : Migration, Xenophobia and Informality in South Africa.)18

[81]Michael J. Schultheis(1989)(Journal Refugees in Africa: The Geopolitics of Forced Displacement) African Studies Review (Online) (Vol. 32, No. 1) (Pp. 3-29) Available: https://www.jstor.org/stable/524491 Accessed : 04/01/21

[82]Crush, Jonathan, Chikanda, Abel, and Skinner, Caroline,(eds). Mean Streets : Migration, Xenophobia and Informality in South Africa.)49

[83] Neocosmos, Michael. *From Foreign Natives to Native Foreigners : Explaining Xenophobia in Post-Apartheid South Africa.* Dakar: CODESRIA 2010)

[84]Neocosmos, Michael. *From Foreign Natives to Native Foreigners : Explaining Xenophobia in Post-Apartheid South Africa. Dakar: CODESRIA* 2010)94

[85]Kevin Durrheim. *Race Trouble : Race, Identity and Inequality in Post-Apartheid South Africa.* (Lanham, MD: Lexington Books. 2011)9

[86] Finley, Mary Lou, LaFayette, Bernard, Jr., Ralph, James R., Jr., and Smith, Pam, eds. *The Chicago Freedom*

Movement : Martin Luther King Jr. and Civil Rights Activism in the North. Lexington: University Press of Kentucky.2016)237

[87]Yanco, Jennifer J... Misremembering Dr. King : Revisiting the Legacy of Martin Luther King Jr.)53

[88]Warren Cohen I.. *Profiles in Humanity : The Battle for Peace, Freedom, Equality, and Human Rights.* Lanham, MD: Rowman & Littlefield Publishers. 2009.)7

[89] Merlene V. Reid . .(2014) (Perspective Transformation Theory and the Donald Woods Experience From Racist to Anti-Apartheid Activist). Prejudice Reduction and Transformation theory (OnlinePaper)Available:https://digitalcommons.fiu.edu/cgi/viewcontent.cgi?article=1347&context=sfec. Accessed:11/01/2021

[90] Galatians 3:29-29

[91] Merlene V. Reid .(2014) (Perspective Transformation Theory and the Donald Woods Experience From Racist to Anti-Apartheid Activist). Prejudice Reduction and Transformation theory (OnlinePaper)Available:https://digitalcommons.fiu.edu/cgi/viewcontent.cgi?article=1347&context=sfec. Accessed:11/01/2021

[92]Keri E. Revens, Andrew D. Reynolds, Roger F. Suclupe, Cameron Rifkin & Taylor Pierce (2018) "You can never understand a culture until you experience it": Journal of Teaching in Social Work,(Online) (Pp 277-291,Available: https://doi.org/10.1080/08841233.2018.1460289
Accessed: 23/01/2021

[93] Alan E Steinweis and Robert Rachlin. *The Law in Nazi Germany* .Berghan Books. New York 2013)6

[94] Robert P.Gordon. *The God of Israel*.(Cambridge University Press 2007)3

[95] David Guzik(2020),(enduring Word Bible Commentary Philippians)(OnlineBible Commentary) Available: https://enduringword.com/bible-commentary/Exodus-3/ Accessed 12/01/2021

[96] Exodus 3:7

[97]David Guzik(2020),(enduring Word Bible Commentary Philippians)(OnlineBible Commentary) Available: https://enduringword.com/bible-commentary/Exodus-3/ Accessed 12/01/2021

[98] David Guzik(2020),(enduring Word Bible Commentary Philippians)(OnlineBible Commentary) Available: https://enduringword.com/bible-commentary/Exodus-3/ Accessed 12/01/21

[99]Jim Myers,. *Afraid of the Dark : What Whites and Blacks Need to Know about Each Other*. Chicago: Lawrence Hill Books. 2000)107

[100]John 1:46

[101]Myers, Jim.. *Afraid of the Dark : What Whites and Blacks Need to Know about Each Other*. Chicago: Lawrence Hill Books.200)113

[102]Paul Bramadat and Lorne Dawson ,*Religious radicalization in Canada and beyond*, (University Of Toronto Press 2014)8

[103] Elijah Anderson *Code of the Street Decency, Violence and the Moral life of the Inner city* (W.W. Norton and Company Ltd .London 2000)11

[104] Glenn Erwin Jackson *Surviving the radicalization of America* (iUniverse Lincoln 2005)11

[105] Rosemary Henze, Anne Katz Edmundo Norte, Susan E Sather and Ernest Walker. *Leading For Diversity* 22.

[106] Rosemary Henze, Anne Katz Edmundo Norte, Susan E Sather and Ernest Walker. *Leading For Diversity* 21-22

[107] Rosemary Henze, Anne Katz Edmundo Norte, Susan E Sather and Ernest Walker. Leading For Diversity (Sage Publications Company. London 2002)22

[108] Paul Kivel, *Uprooting racism* . (New society Publishers .Canada 2011)4

[109] Paul Kivel, *Uprooting racism* . (New society Publishers .Canada 2011)44

[110] Paul Kivel, *Uprooting racism* . (New society Publishers .Canada 2011)44

[111] Freeman O. Ileyemi *The power of Purpose* (Page Publishing Inc. New York 2016)11

[112] Bay, and Bay, Mia. *The White Image in the Black Mind : African-American Ideas about White People, 1830-1925.* New York: Oxford University Press 2000)17

[113] Bay, and Bay, Mia. *The White Image in the Black Mind : African-American Ideas about White People, 1830-1925.* 2000)21

[114]Bay, and Bay, Mia. *The White Image in the Black Mind : African-American Ideas about White People, 1830-1925.* 2000)26

[115]Freeman O. Ileyemi The power of Purpose (Page Publishing Inc. New York 2016)11

[116]Paul Kivel, *Uprooting racism* . (New society Publishers .Canada 2011)55
[117]Paul Kivel, *Uprooting racism* . (New society Publishers .Canada 2011)56

[118]Paul Kivel, *Uprooting racism* . (New society Publishers .Canada 2011)56

[119]Yanco, Jennifer J... *Misremembering Dr. King : Revisiting the Legacy of Martin Luther King Jr.*)51

[120]Gavan Titley and Alana Lentin(eds) ,*The Politics of Diversity in Europe.*(Council of Europe Publishing 2008) 31

[121]David Hoffman, John Jermyn Rowe · *Human Rights in the UK, An introduction to the Human Rights Act 1998* (Pearson Education Limited .Essex 2006) 24

[122]Rosalind Millam. Anti-discriminatory Practice (Continuum London 2002)24

[123]Yvonne Nolan S/NVQ Level 3 .*Health And Social Care* British Library Heinemann.Debby 2006) 176

[124]Peter Morey and Amina Yaqin. *Framing Muslims : Stereotyping and Representation after 9/11.* Cambridge: Harvard University Press.2011)44

[125] Peter Morey and Amina Yaqin. *Framing Muslims : Stereotyping and Representation after 9/11.* Cambridge: Harvard University Press.2011)13

[126] Brent Massey.*Where In the World Do I belong.*(UK Jetlag press 2006)11

[127] Rosalind Millam. *Anti-discriminatory Practice* (Continuum London 2002)28

[128] Rosalind Millam. *Anti-discriminatory Practice* (Continuum London 2002) viii

[129] Rosalind Millam. *Anti-discriminatory Practice* (Continuum London 2002) x-ix

[130] Rosalind Millam. *Anti-discriminatory Practice* (Continuum London 2002)19

[131] Bay, and Bay, Mia. *The White Image in the Black Mind : African-American Ideas about White People, 1830-1925.* New York: Oxford University Press,2000)4

[132] Bay, and Bay, Mia. *The White Image in the Black Mind : African-American Ideas about White People, 1830-1925.* 2000)19

[133] Bay, and Bay, Mia. *The White Image in the Black Mind : African-American Ideas about White People, 1830-1925.* 2000)20

[134] Bay, and Bay, Mia. *The White Image in the Black Mind : African-American Ideas about White People, 1830-1925.* 2000)4

Bay, and Bay, Mia. *The White Image in the Black Mind : African-American Ideas about White People, 1830-1925.* New York: Oxford University Press,2000)22

[135]Bay, and Bay, Mia. *The White Image in the Black Mind : African-American Ideas about White People, 1830-1925.* 2000)24

[136]Yvonne Nolan 2006)196

[137]Yvonne Nolan 2006)196

[138] Neil Thompson. *Anti-Discriminatory Practice: Equality, Diversity and Social Justice* Palgrave .UK 2016)8

[139]Prov 23:7

[140]Neil Thompson. *Anti-Discriminatory Practice: Equality, Diversity and Social Justice* Palgrave .UK 2016)5

[141]Yvonne Nolan 2006)177

[142] Neil Thompson *Anti-Discriminatory Practice: Equality, Diversity and Social Justice* Palgrave .UK 2016)2

[143]Neil Thompson. *Anti-Discriminatory Practice: Equality, Diversity and Social Justice* Palgrave .UK 2016)2

[144]Neil Thompson. Anti-Discriminatory Practice: Equality, Diversity and Social Justice Palgrave .UK 2016)7

[145]Neil Thompson. *Anti-Discriminatory Practice: Equality, Diversity and Social Justice* Palgrave .UK 2016)10

[146] Kevin Durrheim *Race Trouble : Race, Identity and Inequality in Post-Apartheid South Africa.* Lanham, MD: Lexington Books. 2011)17

[147] United Nations, (Peace, Dignity,and Equality on a healthy planet) Online Article. Available: https://www.un.org/en/site-index accessed:27/09/2021

[148] Kevin Durrheim *Race Trouble : Race, Identity and Inequality in Post-Apartheid South Africa.* 2011)17

[149] Durrheim, Kevin. *Race Trouble : Race, Identity and Inequality in Post-Apartheid South Africa.* Lanham, MD: Lexington Books 2011)19

[150] Bay, and Bay, Mia. *The White Image in the Black Mind : African-American Ideas about White People, 1830-1925.* New York: Oxford University Press,2000)27,28

Bibliography

Anderson Elijah Code of the Street Decency, Violence and the Moral life of the Inner city (W.W. Norton and Company Ltd .London 2000)11

Glenn Erwin Jackson Surviving the radicalization of America (iUniverse Lincoln 2005)11

Al Gini and Green Ronald . (25 March 2013) Abraham Lincoln/Rosa Parks: Moral.Wiley online library Available: https://doi-org.dtl.idm.oclc.org/10.1002/9781118551653.ch7 Accessed: 10/01/2021

Bay, and Mia Bay. The White Image in the Black Mind : African-American Ideas about White People, 1830-1925. New York: Oxford University Press,2000)27,28

Borman, Kathryn M., and Dorn, Sherma (eds. Education Reform in Florida : Diversity and Equity in Public Policy. Ithaca: State University of New York Press. 2007)10

Bramadat Paul and Dawson Lorne ,Religious radicalization in Canada and beyond, (University Of Toronto Press 2014)8

Byrne Bridget, Alexander Claire, Omar Khan, Nazro James and Shankley William Ethnicity and Race in the UK: State of the Nation (Bristol University Press, Policy Press 2020)10

Cohen Warren I.. Profiles in Humanity : The Battle for Peace, Freedom, Equality, and Human Rights. Lanham, MD: Rowman & Littlefield Publishers. 2009.)7

Crush, Jonathan, Chikanda, Abel, and Skinner, Caroline, eds. Mean Streets : Migration, Xenophobia and Informality in South Africa. Cape Town: (Southern African Migration Programme (SAMP)2015)5.

Durrheim Kevin Race Trouble : Race, Identity and Inequality in Post-Apartheid South Africa. Lanham, MD: Lexington Books. 2011)17

Ferdinand Keith (M.D).,Tivona Batieste and Mashl iFleurestil (M.S).(June 2020)(Contemporary and Future Concepts on Hypertension in African

Fredrickson, George M., and Fredrickson, George M..Big Enough to Be Inconsistent : Abraham Lincoln Confronts Slavery and Race. Cambridge: Harvard University Press.2008)18

Americans: COVID-19 and Beyond. Journal of the National Medical Association. Online (Volume 112, Issue 3,) (Pages 315-323) Available: https://doi.org/10.1016/j.jnma.2020.05.018 Accessed: 02/01/2021

Gentleman Amelia. The Windrush Betrayal.(Bloomsbury House. London 2019)1-5

Gillespie Michele, and McMillen, Sally G., eds. North Carolina Women : Their Lives and Times, Volume 2. Athens: University of Georgia Press.2015)263

Gordon Robert P.. The God of Israel.(Cambridge University Press 2007)3

Goodfellow Maya Hostile Environment, How immigrants became scapegoats (Veso Books. London.2019)50

Guzik David (2020),(enduring Word Bible Commentary Philippians)(OnlineBible Commentary) Available: https://enduringword.com/bible-commentary/Exodus-3/ Accessed 12/01/2021

Henze Rosemary, Katz Anne, Norte Edmundo, Sathe Susan E r and Walker Ernest. Leading For Diversity 22.

Hoffman David , Rowe John Jermyn • Human Rights in the UK, An introduction to the Human Rights Act 1998 (Pearson Education Limited .Essex 2006) 24

Holzera Harry J. and Reaser Jess (Nov 200)(Black Applicants, Black Employees, and Urban Labor Market Policy) Journal of Urban Economics Online:(Volume 48, Issue 3,) (Pp 365-387) Available: https://doi.org/10.1006/juec.2000.2171
Accesed:02/01/2021

Hung Pal Hsiao –and Zephaniah Benjamin,Angry White People.(Zed Books Limited .London.2016) Preview

Ileyomi Freeman O. The power of Purpose (Page Publishing Inc. New York 2016)11

Kane, John. The Politics of Moral Capital. (Cambridge: Cambridge University Press.2001)149

Kivel Paul, Uprooting racism . (New society Publishers .Canada 2011)44
The New Strategist Editors, ed. Racial and Ethnic Diversity : Asians, Blacks, Hispanics, Native Americans and Whites. (Amityville: New Strategist Press,2013)2

Kintsurashvil Tamar i , Ratiani Maiko 30 April 2020 Does Bill Gates promise us depopulation and chipping? Healthcare/Biosafety Online article .Available: http://www.mythdetector.ge/en/myth/does-bill-gates-promise-us-depopulation-and-chipping Accessed: 12/01/2021

Kuhl, Stefan. The Nazi Connection : Eugenics, American Racism, and German National Socialism. Cary: Oxford University Press,2002)xiv

Likupe Gloria PhD, MSc, PGCEA, BSc (Hons), DipN, RN Uduak Archibong PhD, FWACN, FRCN(Black African Nurses' Experiences of Equality, Racism, and Discrimination in the National Health Service)(Psychological issues in Organisational culture) Wiley Online Library (Oneline)Journal.(Volume3, IssueS1)(Pages 227-246) Available:(https://doi.org/10.1002/jpoc.21071) accessed:14/11/20

Lockwood Graeme , Henderson Claire and Thornicroft Graham (March 2012)(Article/equality-act-2010-and-mental-health) The British Journal of Psychiatry (Online)(Volume 200 , Issue 3,(pp. 182 – 183)Available:DOI: https://doi.org/10.1192/bjp.bp.111.097790) accessed: 01/01/2021

Lou Finley, , LaFayette Mary, Ralph Bernard, Jr.,R. James Jr, and Smith Pam, eds. The Chicago Freedom Movement : Martin Luther King Jr. and Civil Rights Activism in the North. Lexington: University Press of Kentucky.2016)237

Massey Brent.Where In the World Do I belong.(UK Jetlag press 2006)11

Millam Rosalind. Anti-discriminatory Practice (Continuum London 2002)28

Malloy Sean L. Out of Oakland : Black Panther Party Internationalism during the Cold War. Ithaca: Cornell University Press. 2017)241

Matondi, Prosper B... Zimbabwe's Fast Track Land Reform.(London: Zed Books. 2012)xi

Marovich Pete (06/01/21) (The Presidential Transition)The New York Times Online . Available: https://www.nytimcs.com/2021/01/06/us/politics/trump-speech-capitol.html Accessed: 08/01/21

Memmi Albert. Racism. (Minneapolis: University of Minnesota Press 1999)10

Morey Peter and Yaqin Amina . Framing Muslims : Stereotyping and Representation after 9/11. Cambridge: Harvard University Press.2011)44

Mostern Kenneth . Autobiography and Black Identity Politics : Racialization in Twentieth-Century America. Cambridge: Cambridge University Press.1999)149

Moyo, Sam, and Chambati, Walter, eds. (Land and Agrarian Reform in Zimbabwe : Beyond White-Settler Capitalism. Dakar: CODESRIA 2013)30

Myers Jim,. Afraid of the Dark : What Whites and Blacks Need to Know about Each Other. Chicago: Lawrence Hill Books. 2000)107

Neocosmos Michael. From Foreign Natives to Native Foreigners : Explaining Xenophobia in Post-Apartheid South Africa. Dakar: CODESRIA 2010)

Nolan Yvonne S/NVQ Level 3 .Health And Social Care British Library Heinemann.Debby 2006) 176

O Dyer.(07 September 2020) (Covid-19: Black people and other minorities are hardest hit in US).The journal of rural health.Online:(Volume36, Issue4) (Pp 602-608)Available: https://doi.org/10.1111/jrh.12511 Accessed:02/01/2021

Pendleton John (The experiences of black and minority ethnic nurses working in the UK) British Journal of Nursing (Jan 2017) (Online) (VOL. 26, NO. 1) Available: https://doi.org/10.12968/bjon.2017.26.1.37 Accessed:14/11/20

Prejudice Reduction and Transformation theory (OnlinePaper)Available:https://digitalcommons.fiu.edu/cgi/viewcontent.cgi?article=1347&context=sfec. Accessed:11/01/2021

. Reid Merlene V. .(2014) (Perspective Transformation Theory and the Donald Woods Experience From Racist to Anti-Apartheid Activist).

Revens Keri E., . Reynolds Andrew D, . Suclupe Roger F, Cameron Rifkin & Taylor Pierce (2018) "You can never understand a culture until you experience it": Journal of Teaching in Social Work,(Online) (Pp 277-291,Available:
https://doi.org/10.1080/08841233.2018.1460289
Accessed: 23/01/2021

Rosario Rodriguez, Ruben.Racism and God-Talk: A Latino/a Perspective.(NYU Press, 2008)1

Schultheis Michael J. (1989)(Journal Refugees in Africa: The Geopolitics of Forced Displacement) African Studies Review (Online) (Vol. 32, No. 1) (Pp. 3-29) Available: https://www.jstor.org/stable/524491 Accessed : 04/01/21

Smith Ben Riley, Sabur Rozina and Allen Nick. (8 January 2021) Five dead in US Capitol riot after Donald Trump's supporters storm Washington) USA, (US Election, US Politics, Donald Trump The telegraph, Online, available : https://www.telegraph.co.uk/news/2021/01/08/us-capitol-riot-protest-what-happened-who-died-trump-supporters/ Accessed :08/01/21

Steinweis Alan E and Rachlin Robert. The Law in Nazi Germany .Berghan Books. New York 2013)6

Stearnsa Elizabeth , Jhaa Nandan and Potochnick Stephanie (Race, secondary school course of study, and college type)May 2013 Social Science Research.Online (Volume 42, Issue 3) (Pages 789-803) Available: https://doi.org/10.1016/j.ssresearch.2013.01.007 Accessed:02/01/2021

Sood Lakshay Sood Vanita (MD) (03 May 2020) (Being African American and Rural: A Double Jeopardy From COVID-19) The journal of Rural Health Online (Volume37, Issue1) (Pp 217-221) Available: https://doi.org/10.1111/jrh.12459 Accessed: 02/01/2021

Taylor, Yamahtta Keeanga-. From #BlackLivesMatter to Black Liberation. (Chicago: Haymarket Books.2016)4

Theoharis Jeanne, The Rebellious Life of Mrs. Rosa Parks (Beacon Press Massachusetts 2013)x

Thompson Neil. Anti-Discriminatory Practice: Equality, Diversity and Social Justice Palgrave .UK 2016)10

Titley Gavan and Lentin Alana (eds) ,The Politics of Diversity in Europe.(Council of Europe Publishing 2008) 31

Warren Cohen I. Profiles in Humanity : The Battle for Peace, Freedom, Equality, and Human Rights. (Lanham, MD: Rowman & Littlefield Publishers.2009)134

Warren Rueben C., D.D.S., Dr.P.H., M.Div., Forrow Lachlan, M.D., Augustin David Hodge, Sr., D.Min., Ph.D., and Robert D. Truog, M.D. 16 Oct 2020 Trustworthiness before Trust — Covid-19 Vaccine Trials and the Black The New England Journal of Medicine (Online) Available: https://www.nejm.org/doi/full/10.1056/NEJMp2030033 Accessed: 12/01/2021

Webster Colin Understanding Race and Crime. Buckingham: McGraw-Hill Education. 2007)3

Wojciech Piontek 2019 Depopulation in the Concept of Sustainable Development Middle Pomeranian scientific Society Of Environment Protection Rocznik Ochrona
Środowiska (Online) Paper Volume 21 (Pp 523-542 Available: https://ros.edu.pl/images/roczniki/2019/032_ROS_V21_R 2019.pdf Accessed:12/01/2021

Yanco, Jennifer J... Misremembering Dr. King : Revisiting the Legacy of Martin Luther King)54

Zamalin, Alex. Struggle on Their Minds : The Political Thought of African American Resistance. New York: Columbia University Press.2017)120

www.ingramcontent.com/pod-product-compliance
Lightning Source LLC
Chambersburg PA
CBHW071518220526
45472CB00003B/1067